FIGHT TO WIN

Chris Ryan was born near Newcastle in 1961. He joined the SAS in 1984 and was a member for ten years. During the Gulf War, Chris was the only member of an eight-man team to escape from Iraq, of which three colleagues were killed and four captured. It was the longest escape and evasion in the history of the SAS. For his last two years he was selecting and training potential recruits for the SAS.

He is a bestselling author and lectures in business motivation and security. He is currently working as a bodyguard in America.

CHRIS RYAN

FIGHT TO WIN

arrow books

Published in the United Kingdom by Arrow Books in 2010

1 3 5 7 9 10 8 6 4 2

First published in Great Britain in 2009 by Century

Arrow Books
Random House
20 Vauxhall Bridge Road, London SW1V 2SA

Addresses for companies within The Random House Group Limited
can be found at: www.randomhouse.co.uk/offices.htm

The Random House Group Limited Reg. No. 954009
www.rbooks.co.uk

A CIP catalogue record for this book is available from the British Library

ISBN 9780099539322

The Random House Group Limited supports The Forest Stewardship
Council (FSC), the leading international forest certification organisation.
All our titles that are printed on Greenpeace approved FSC certified paper
carry the FSC logo. Our paper procurement policy can be found at
www.rbooks.co.uk/environment

Mixed Sources
Product group from well-managed
forests and other controlled sources
www.fsc.org Cert no. TT-COC-2139
© 1996 Forest Stewardship Council
FSC

Design/typesetting by Roger Walker

Printed and bound in Great Britain by
CPI Bookmarque Ltd, Croydon, CR0 4TD

CONTENTS

INTRODUCTION

> WHAT IT MEANS TO BE AN ELITE OPERATOR //

 **Being a Special Forces soldier is about more than being a skilled warrior. It's about being the best – and believing you are.**

No one is told to be an elite operator – everyone volunteers. That's important because to be a successful operator you need to have the desire and determination to do it, and that is something that comes from within. Being able to walk hundreds of miles when you're cold, hungry and tired requires an inner resolve and self-belief that is unique to each individual who volunteers for service. It's the same whether you're an SAS or SBS operator or Para or Marine.

When I was in the SAS we were told, 'Don't fail in anything'. That's not true, of course – no one can succeed in everything they do – but it was an important lesson about the value of self-belief. You have to believe you can push yourself beyond the limits of normal human endurance and survive outside the comfort zone. You need a special determination to survive against the odds in inhospitable environments, carrying out missions against a much larger enemy force or evading capture when the Iraqi army is hunting you down.

In the Regiment, we always thought we were better than anyone else. That, more than the incredibly tough training and advanced skills we were taught, helped us get through when the going got tough.

Recently I was lucky enough to work with some of the world's elite police forces for my TV show. Although units like Poland's BOA and Sri Lanka's Special Task Force are elite paramilitary police units rather than Special Forces teams, much of the training they have is similar, and many of the teams, including the Sri Lankans, were in fact created by colleagues of mine from the SAS. They work in brutal environments, on the frontline of the war on crime, taking on gangsters and guerrilla armies in challenging circumstances.

None of the guys is there because he was told to – just like the guys in the SAS, they volunteered for a much tougher job than regular police work, for not much more money, and with all the professional and personal risks the work brings.

These guys all did it for the same reason: they genuinely want to make their countries a better place to live. Being a great elite operator is about more than being the fittest soldier or the best rifle shot – although it helps to be both. You have to be a great team player as well as a great individual. When the team works, the team wins.

Chris Ryan
September 2009

01 SELECTION

> **SPECIAL FORCES SOLDIERS HAVE EARNED THEIR REPUTATION AS BEING THE TOUGHEST AND SHARPEST IN THE BUSINESS. AND IN TODAY'S WORLD, THEY PLAY A CRUCIAL ROLE IN WINNING BATTLES AND WARS – ARGUABLY THE MOST IMPORTANT ROLE OF ALL //**

I recently found myself working alongside the Jungla commandos in war-torn Colombia. The Junglas are tough guys; they're trained in reconnaissance, infiltration and assault, with the aim of defeating the evil drug lords responsible for the country's appalling state. Jungla commandos often survive for weeks in the jungle, and they're pretty effective at what they do (although I'd choose the Special Air Service over them any day of the week).

What surprised me most was that these guys are supposed to be police officers, not soldiers. But they're not your average plod. They are heavily influenced by Special Forces – particularly my mates in the SAS, who originally trained the Junglas before handing the show over to the Americans. Sometimes they're a bit too eager, which is probably down to the Yanks.

But the Junglas show how, these days, the techniques of the Special Forces underpins much regular military and even civilian defence thinking. And that's because the fighting techniques they employ are uniquely effective.

The SAS is the original and still the best Special Forces team in the world. We're feared and respected across the board, and many of the special fighting techniques and training methods we have developed and perfected down the years are practised and replicated in a lot of other fighting forces – although none of them does it quite as well as the lads in Hereford. When Winston Churchill introduced the concept of Special Forces (SF) commandos in the Second World War, the success of these special ops in Occupied Europe, North Africa and the Middle East helped to turn the tide against Hitler. Other armies noted the success of 22 SAS, as well as other units such as the SBS and the Special Operations Executive (SOE). The US Army's Rangers and Marine Corps, and the Navy SEALS, were all influenced by British SF.

Some – such as Sayeret Matkal in Israel and the Australian SAS – even use the same motto as the Regiment: 'Who Dares Wins'. Today, SAS techniques are taught by soldiers, both serving and former, to other Special Forces, Armed Forces and even police units, from Australia to Brazil to Singapore. Some of the Regiment's operations have gone down in history as military legend – including my own Bravo Two Zero mission in Iraq. This book, in part, is a testament to the legacy of the SAS.

But to be in any Special Forces team, whether it's the SAS or the Navy Seals or whoever, requires exceptional soldiers. You have to be extremely physically fit, at the same level as a boxer like Joe Calzaghe or a footballer like Steven Gerrard. You've also got to be sharp, intelligent, have good instincts and be able to think quickly whilst under extreme pressure. And even when you're in deep trouble, hungry, tired, cold and being pursued by the enemy, you have to stay focused on the task in hand.

What the task is depends on the nature of the mission and of the type of Special Forces unit involved. It could be an Army force, like the SAS or the American Green Berets, spending a prolonged time behind enemy lines on a vital recce mission. Or it could be a

Navy SF team like our very own SAS Boat Troop and Special Boat Service (SBS), targeting merchant warships. Increasingly, covert ops are on the rise, with intelligence organisations like the Israeli Mossad using ex-soldiers to carry out assassinations.

But whatever SF unit we're talking about, the same basic principle applies: if you don't prepare properly, you're asking for trouble. Or, put it another way: **fail to prepare, prepare to fail**.

In most cases, any regular serving soldier can apply to join Special Forces units. Historically, it has been common for soldiers with an airborne background to apply for SF selection. Special Forces operators need Special Forces training, because in regular Armed Forces, those units are regarded as the most demanding, physically, and the parachute experience comes in handy when it comes to practising high-altitude freefalls. A lot of soldiers from the Parachute regiments in England, like the famous 2 and 3 Para, go on to try their hands at Selection. There's no doubt they are already in top physical condition, and that this gives them an advantage in some parts of the selection process. But there's also a lot more to SF techniques than brawn: you need brains as well. In my experience, the regular squaddies who think they're

Superman tend to struggle with the rigorous demands of SAS training. It's called 'dumb muscle' for a reason. So coming from a tough guy background isn't *always* best. One of the reasons why the Regiment is so respected is because we take an unorthodox approach to selection: engineers, signals specialists, military police, medics, guys from intelligence units, even chefs — we encourage anyone from a different background to apply, because the specialist skills they bring to the table are often invaluable. After all, you can teach the nuclear engineer to pack on a few pounds of muscle; it can be a lot tougher trying to teach the Para sharp shooter how to speak Arabic.

To begin with, you need to make sure whatever soldiers, from whichever background you are selecting for your SF team, are good enough to cope with the demands of working for a highly sophisticated outfit. That's where Selection comes in. Part of the reason why SAS soldiers are respected and feared the world over is because Selection is so demanding.

SAS SELECTION

Twice a year the SAS runs its Selection camp. In my later years in the Regiment I was a Selection instructor – in fact, every instructor who runs Selection is a full member of the Regiment. Knowing what it takes to be a Blade is an important part of being able to identify those who have the ability to join the hallowed ranks.

Up to two hundred men take part in Selection, in a programme that lasts five weeks. Selection is open to all three services, including the Territorial Army SAS. The SAS is the only regiment that does not recruit directly from the general public, and Selection is the main reason why. Only around ten will actually be selected for SAS service at the end of it – sometimes less depending on the instructor and the standard of the guys.

At the start candidates are taken to Sennybridge in Powys, a rural community in the Brecon Beacons. Here they will undergo a Battle Fitness Test (BFT) and a Combat Fitness Test (CFT). Candidates must prove themselves across a series of tabs (cross-country route marches) in the Brecon Beacons and Black Mountains of South Wales (including a vomit-inducing twenty-three kilometre march, with full gear, up the Fan Dance, or to give it its real name, Pen-y-Fan, and against the clock to boot). You have around four hours to complete this. By the end of this first phase, the soldiers must be able to walk four miles in less than half an hour, as well as swimming two miles in ninety minutes. The course places heavy emphasis on land navigation ability and gets soldiers thinking and performing outside the box: for each day, they are given a rendezvous (RV) point and told to get on with the job. The location is established, but how they get there is up to them. The soldiers aren't even given an expected reporting time, they're just told 'Get there as quick as you can' – they have no idea whether their best is quick enough or not. All these elements sow the seeds of doubt in the mind of the candidate. You have to have extreme mental resilience and self-belief to make it through. This open-ended approach also forces the soldiers to adapt to their environment and make quick, sound field decisions based on the environment, their resources and the objective. I've heard of some very good, professional soldiers freaking out when being told to work outside the structure of regular military units, where they're told how and when to tie their bootlaces. The instructors will be silent – they won't shout, criticise or give encouragement to the candidates. This silence is very different from the treatment they get in their parent regiments, where they are used to being told how well or badly they are doing, and again you need to be mentally tough enough to carry out the tasks without any motivation.

For soldiers who don't feel that the SAS is for them, they can 'rap' out of the process at any time. In my day we had a bucket in the barracks. If you wanted to give up, you had to pick up the bucket. If you do rap, you'll get another chance. Actually a lot of guys come in for a second go.

After the Hill phase there is the jungle phase, where students learn about how to hold, strip and use a weapon. This might seem a bit strange, teaching career soldiers how to fire guns, but some students will come from non-firearms backgrounds, maybe as engineers or cooks, and in Selection it's important that all the students are given a fair crack of the whip – no one has an unfair advantage over anybody else.

The best way of holding a weapon depends on the combat situation confronting the operator. Lying face down in the prone position gives the soldier the best cover and protection but renders him immobile. In contrast, the kneeling position gives the operator a good balance between stability and cover, enabling him to lay down rounds effectively. Standing fully upright is risky because it leaves the soldier highly exposed and is best used when there is some cover available such as trees. They are also taught the principle of sustained fire (SF) – namely that, if you

It's important for instructors not to be too harsh on candidates. When I was an instructor I always said my job was to pass people, not fail them.

have your enemy pinned down with constant gunfire, it's going to be difficult for him to operate weaponry or detonate explosives.

Entering the jungle the team is inserted straight under the canopies. The Regiment uses Belize, Brunei and Malaysia for jungle training, because each represents a different type of jungle. Brunei is primary jungle, where the trees are tall and form two or three canopies at the top, blocking out natural light. The undergrowth is very clean, similar to an English forest, although it is very dark and visibility can be down to 10 metres at ridge ends and just a couple of metres near river ends. In Belize the terrain is known as 'dirty' or secondary jungle. Here the primary trees have been cut down allowing the undergrowth to flourish, making it very difficult to move around. It's so thick that it's really hard to walk through and is a great place for testing the guys' ability. Hacking their way through is sometimes an option, but this is noisy and leaves evidence of the patrol's movement, so where possible they will try to navigate around it, as well as overcoming 'wait-a-while bushes' – rattan and climbing palms that rip at your clothes if you get caught up on them so you have to wait a while to untangle from them! Imagine a 100-metres thick bramble bush that you have to try and get through!

The easiest way to move through heavy undergrowth is up high on the ridge lines, but these are used by animals (who can make noises when they encounter man thus alerting nearby enemy soldiers) and also the enemy team that is being tracked by the patrol. The students will instead walk using a technique called cross-graining, where you walk up and down over the ridges.

Before the students land an advance party will go out and locate a Landing Zone (LZ). They'll look for a dirty, wet, horrible slab of jungle for the students to camp out In, to weed out those who can't tolerate living in terrible conditions for long periods of time.

All the technical lessons a student needs are taught here: navigation (a vital skill for elite forces operating in environments that lack landmarks or distinguishing features such as the jungle and desert), how to look through different layers of canopy to identify targets and the principles of Why Things Are Seen – Shape, Shine, Silhouette, Shadow, Spacing, Movement (I'll talk about these in more detail later).

Students are also taught how to move in patrol formation in primary and secondary jungle. The guys will move in single file. The distance between each man depends very much on the visibility of the terrain. On a clear ridge the guys will spread out to a distance of about 10-15 metres between each other, but down below in dirty jungle undergrowth in a tight bush area, that distance will reduce down to 2 or 3 metres. The range expands and contracts depending on terrain and visibility.

Students are also taught to communicate in hand signals only. If you do need to talk for whatever reason, you step off the ridge line, do a loop, set up shop and the patrol commander then talks to the team if necessary.

Surviving in the jungle can be a harsh, isolated experience. A lot of the guys go into the jungle shaven-headed for hygiene purposes, healthy and with a tan – and when they emerge four weeks later, they all have unkempt beards, gaunt, pale faces and unruly hair.

During jungle training the students will also be taught harbour routines. Patrol harbours are temporary field HQs that allow elite operators to conduct campaigns whilst detached from the main armed forces. I'll talk about this in more detail later. Choosing a spot for the night they will have to make up a hammock (lying on

There are countless times I was on jungle patrol when not a word was spoken for several weeks. The only talk might be a quickly whispered word or two at first light on stand-to, after we'd packed away our ponchos and had a kip. Not speaking is horrible, you're under arduous conditions, sweating, knackered, carrying heavy weight, you have got to have your wits about you constantly, and sometimes you want to sit and chat, to ease some of the pain, but you know you can't. It plays on your mind.

the ground would disturb the soil and vegetation and alert enemy trackers), tying it round the trees with a bit of hessian cloth to avoid leaving marks on them. Waking up one hour before first light, everybody packs up and moves off at daybreak.

The team then dosses up in an ambush position, gets some boil-in-the-bag foods down them – anything from chicken curry to beef hash, beef stew, beans or sausages. They will then scout for enemy forces (played by a local Gurkha regiment. In my day they were shipped over from Hong Kong but today some Gurkhas are based in Brunei). The students have the choice of launching an ambush or allowing the enemy to walk past them, bugging out and legging it.

An hour before last light they send a signal back to base and eat again. During darkness, the students look for somewhere to pitch up for the night. They will pay close attention to the tree canopies, where the possibility of deadfall (loose branches falling on the soldiers and crushing them) is a constant threat. Even whole trees can collapse on a soldier, as jungle trees sometimes have very shallow root systems.

The difference between the students who survive the jungle phase and those who do not is discipline. You have to be disciplined at all times, making sure you remove your wet clothes at night, powder off, sleep in your dry clothes, then put your wet clothes on again the next morning. It's important to sleep in dry clothes because when you're operating in a hostile environment that requires great physical and mental strength you need a good night's kip at the end of it. Changing clothes also prevents trench foot, a condition that occurs when feet are immersed in cold water, causing the foot to turn numb. If left untreated, it can quickly turn gangrenous and there are horror stories of guys having a foot amputated because they didn't change their socks.

During their time in the jungle the students will also attend classes at a school house, receiving lessons in RV tactics, caching drills, navigation, shooting, and camp attacks, where they must set up an Observation Post (OP) to carry out surveillance on a constructed camp and plan an attack. We will return to techniques like these later in the book.

Once the jungle phase is over students then return to Hereford where they learn about battle plans, get to use foreign weapons on the range (a key skill of elite operators is the ability to use the weapons of their enemies as well as their own issued guns), and take part in a combat survival exercise. They will learn how to navigate by the stars and moon, how to acquire water in the wild, and other survival skills. By the second week, the students will be knackered, pushed to their physical and mental limits. It's an exhausting process, as they will have to absorb a great deal of information in classes as well as carry out demanding physical exercises. Only the best will survive. Throughout this process, students will be rapping out all the time.

The final exercise involves the remaining students being put into patrols and told to make an escape carrying nothing more than a tin can filled with bits of essential survival gear like razor blades and money. They're dressed in old WWII uniforms, given a sketch map and told to make an RV by first light in a very remote, rural area. They will be on the run, all told, for a week, trying to evade capture by a large hunting force composed of paras and marines that has helicopters, dogs, the lot. At the end of the week, whether they have managed to avoid capture or not, the students who make it to the final RV are loaded onto a cattle truck, tied up and taken to the interrogation centre at Hereford.

The students must now undergo the final part of the Selection test: Resistance to Interrogation (RTI).

During filming of my TV series *Elite World Cops*, I got to see the training and drills for some of the world's top paramilitary units. Having seen their skills and fitness up close and personal, I've no doubt that some of them, the elite of the elites, would be capable of passing Selection.

Resisting interrogation doesn't mean fighting your captors. In the SAS, students who try to fight back against the interrogators will be failed. The key is to stick to your lines, don't reveal any information, and try to be subservient, quiet and even try to establish friendship with your interrogators. It's all about mental strength – the key attribute for any elite operator.

Some people ask how it's possible to replicate interrogation techniques when the student is aware that the situation is staged and that his interrogators aren't the enemy. I would say that, by the time you enter RTI you're exhausted from all the training and a week on the run from tracker teams, you're shattered mentally and physically and in a weak state of mind. You're not really sure if what's going on is real or not. The experience is definitely bewildering. You get a range of interrogators playing all the standard roles – Mr Angry, Mr Friendly, The Woman. They put you in stress positions, such as sitting cross-legged with your hands over your head, or standing with your arms and legs leaning against the wall. If you try and move yourself into a more relaxed position, the interrogators will force you back into the stress pose.

You're also subjected to white noise being pumped at you, and taunts from the Interrogators. RTI lasts for thirty-six hours. At the end you are brought into a room and told that RTI training is over. When you're told this, you're not sure if this is just another part of the game or it is really true. You sit with your mates in this room but no one says a word – there's no back-slapping or anything like that. It's only when the students realise that the game really is over that they can celebrate.

Once the few surviving students have passed Selection they are then transferred to an operational squadron. Importantly, they're not treated as 'the new guy' but just as another one of the lads – expected to muck in and do the same jobs, to the same high standard. Any slacking off or basking in the glory of having an SAS badge will result in the soldier being RTU'd (Returned to Unit). If they're lucky, some of them might even see their first action in a little over a week.

Other elite groups have a different approach to selection, and the demands of a unit can also change over time. Russian elite operators are part of Spetsnaz – not a Special Forces team by itself, but the name given to any elite unit in Russia's military or police (Spetsnaz means 'Special Designation'). Back in the bad old days of the Cold War, military Spetsnaz units were trained for airborne assault and border reconnaissance in a much more traditional army combat role. Today the focus of their operations is very different. The greatest threat to their country is from within, so units like Alpha, responsible for ending the Moscow theatre siege in 2002 are trained in anti-terrorist ops. They have adopted a training regime that focuses on armed responses and gathering intel working in hostile environments such as the Chechnya region.

Selection processes aren't designed to replicate the roles a student will perform in an elite unit – it's impossible to recreate combat conditions. Think of selection tests as markers that will help the instructors see the mental and physical characteristics of the student. I didn't have to travel 300km on foot with no food or water during Selection – but I did display the mental fortitude and discipline which prepared me for Iraq.

The award for the most miserable Selection programme must go to South Africa. Their Special Forces Brigade Selection is famous for its sheer brutality. Potential recruits for the SF unit, known in the trade as the 'Recces', come under fire from live automatic rounds and explosive devices designed to push them to the limit. During exhausting tabs the instructors stand at the checkpoints and take the mick, drinking ice-cold refreshments and tucking into slap-up meals while the exhausted, thirsty recruits struggle to the next RV. That might seem excessive, but then again, they're operating in a blisteringly hot terrain, so there's some logic to this method.

Delta Force applicants place great emphasis on physical training and students will participate in a camp that includes running, swimming and tabs. It's similar to the SAS programme because the guy that created Delta Force, a Colonel by the name of Charles Beckwith in the Green Berets who spent some time on exchange with the SAS in the Sixties, understood that there was no training programme more demanding, more focused, than Selection.

US Army Special Forces have their own programme: Special Forces Assessment and Selection (SFAS), held at Fort Bragg, Northern Carolina. The programme tests leadership skills, physical fitness, motivation and the ability to cope with stress and takes the shape of several cross country courses of distances up to 50 kilometres and requiring land navigation skills. The programme's slogan is that 'Your Mind Is Your Best Weapon' and while I'm tempted to dismiss that as more Yank hype, there's a ring of truth to it: being a perfect physical specimen is simply not enough for the multiple demands of SF operations. I have been on SFAS and it's pretty hard going. The majority of those who apply don't make it through. Fair enough. SF isn't everyone's cup of tea.

A lot of elite selection programmes, such as Delta Force, now include proper psychological profiling and assessments, where doctors fire questions at the soldiers asking them about their family background and views on drugs, religion and foreigners, the idea being that the men in white coats can prevent nut jobs and psychos from joining an elite special ops unit. Personally I'm not convinced that doctors can find out whether a guy is good enough, or mentally sound, for special ops just by asking him a bunch of questions. I'm a great believer in judging people based by what they achieve in the field – you can't

**When I was separated from
my mates in Iraq, I could
have easily given in and
awaited capture. But I didn't.
My training taught me to
stay focused on the objective
and to shut out everything
else – and that ultimately
saved my life.**

replicate the stress and fear of a real combat environment, and certainly not on a multiple-choice questionnaire!

That's why the officers in charge of Selection have an incredibly important job. They are the eyes and ears of the Selection process. They keep a blank expression at all times, no smiles or glares. The instructors are there to observe, not to give encouragement to the candidates. But they do keep a close eye on the soldiers, checking to see if any of them are disruptive presences, as well as looking out for any other tell-tale signs of SF suitability. How they respond to injury and exhaustion is critical: in hostile territory, if you're suffering with a busted ankle, you can't just stop and relax. You have to push on through the pain. There are also mental types of stress that SF commandos need to deal with. For example, because SF units operate In small teams behind enemy lines, the death of a colleague or the separation from the rest of the unit can cause intense mental anguish and trigger a loss of hope. It's up to the soldier to overcome these mental obstacles and remain focused on the mission and survival.

02 TRAINING AND EQUIPMENT

> JUST BECAUSE A STUDENT HAS EARNED A PLACE IN AN ELITE UNIT, DOESN'T MEAN HE CAN REST ON HIS LAURELS //

 Throughout his career in the unit, the elite operator will continue to add more skills, knowledge and training to make sure he and the rest of his unit remain at the very forefront of military warfare.

There are two main aspects to this training: giving soldiers the general tools required to survive and fight as Special Forces commandos; and training them in the specialist skills specific to that unit (e.g. combat divers or demolitions) or theatre of combat – the unit trained in combating the drugs trade in the jungles of South America will need to master different skills to the Arctic patrol protecting the Russian border.

Any SF unit has to divide up certain key skills between different personnel. Generally, the different skill groups are:

MEDICINE // Missions often involve small teams operating in a distant environment, with little if any supplies, in locations crawling with enemy forces. Because the teams are small, they have to be able to absorb injuries to individual members of the patrol and continue operating. And it's not like the guys can just visit the nearest hospital. Medics are therefore crucial to the mission's success. A combat-medicine specialist should know as much as a junior doctor, and in fact as part of their in-depth training, they'll work in cIty hospital trauma units, dealing with bullet and knife wounds, to prepare them for the type of injuries they'll have to address in the field. US Special Forces Medical Sergeants are trained in what is known as 'trauma medicine' – dealing with sometimes horrific injuries and repairing or rehabilitating the soldier with limited kit and in testing conditions. They have to decide, on the spot, who is a priority case and who can carry on fighting – and sometimes make the difficult decision that a soldier's injuries are too severe, and his life cannot be saved. Medical Sergeants also have a good knowledge of dentistry, veterinary care, water quality and optometry.

ENGINEERING // Engineers should be able to construct bridges as well as blown them up. Delta Force commandos will study Explosives Ordnance Disposal (EOD). There are three different gradings: Basic EOD, Master, and Senior. The course teaches Delta soldiers how to build, deploy, disarm and dispose of high explosive munitions, and also covers ordnance types, including NBC (Nuclear, Biological and Chemical) weapons. More recently the focus has switched to IEDs (Improvised Explosive Devices), booby traps that can be hidden or disguised as fizzy drink cans, manholes and even dead animal carcasses. Insurgents are able to detonate them remotely using mobile phones, pagers and even toy car remotes. They have become a commonplace threat to the guys operating in Iraq and Afghanistan.

SIGNALLERS // These lads will be able to operate all forms of communication equipment, including encrypted satellite communications systems, as well as the more old-fashioned Morse code. Some enemy environments are still stuck in the Dark Ages so understanding how out-of-date comms systems operate is vital. But as we are now in a digital world, they need to possess advanced computer programming and networking skills. Signallers need, above all, to be able to quickly learn and master new comms systems. In my day radio systems were heavy and hadn't really changed a lot for many years. Now comms systems are becoming smaller and lighter. These systems are also much more secure. Advances in technology also mean that soldiers can send real-time images of enemy positions to the head shed, allowing military commanders to instantly view the situation on the ground for themselves.

Signals is something that every trooper will be trained in, simply because this is so essential to the success of any Special Forces operation.

LINGUIST // Often SF outfits will be required to fight in combat environments where the language spoken is different to their mother tongue. And it's critical that they are able to communicate with friendly forces, civilians (during escape and evasion manoeuvres or to bribe in exchange for information) and government officials. The local language is also handy when it comes to reading local maps and identifying targets. SAS teams each have a trained linguist who understands the local dialect. Linguist specialists will know several languages, especially those used in more than one country, such as Spanish or French, which are common in Central and South America and East Africa. For missions where the linguist is unfamiliar with the native tongue he will have to commit to memory some basic phrases and key terms, as time is too short to cram in detailed knowledge of the dialect. The other soldiers in the team will also try and bone up on their linguistic skills. Not only is it helpful on the ground to know some useful phrases in, say, Portuguese, it's also vital to the elite operator's career – if he doesn't have some knowledge of foreign languages, that is going to limit the theatres of operation that the head shed will consider inserting him into.

ADMINISTRATION AND INTELLIGENCE //

No SF team can do its job without proper intelligence, and the role of intelligence-gathering has become hugely important in recent years, as governments are faced with a complex network of terrorist cells and guerrilla forces that are more difficult to monitor than traditional armed forces. During my time in the Regiment we had 14 Int – also known as 'The Det' – to help carry out surveillance work for us. They were the masters at being 'the grey man', blending effortlessly into their surrounding environment even while carrying out sensitive surveillance tasks. 14 Int played a key role in Northern Ireland. Now their job is carried out by the Special Reconnaissance Regiment (SRR), whilst 18 (UKSF) Signals Regiment brings together several existing signals regiments and specialises in intercepting radio and mobile phone comms and providing signals intelligence (SIGINT) to SF. These lads also give computer and technology support to the SAS and SBS.

SNIPER // Being a sniper requires different weapon handling skills to other members of a unit. The role of snipers is to gather information about the enemy from concealed surveillance positions, take out vital enemy targets and snipers, and provide accurate support fire for a main assault team. How he achieves this depends on the terrain and the nature of the mission facing him.

Snipers will usually operate in pairs – the idea of a lone sniper taking out targets by himself is pure Hollywood fantasy. By working in pairs they are maximising their chances of taking out the target and keep themselves fresh during often arduous and extensive surveillance of the target. They must also be mobile, able to quickly insert into a combat environment and move easily and effectively through the terrain to locate good firing positions and extract from them, minimising their chances of detection.

When I was an instructor in the Regiment I would get the lads to use anemometers like the ones employed on yachts, to get a reading on wind speed. The guys would then be taught to consult a chart that would tell you how many clicks to adjust fire, based on the wind speed and distance, and the lay of the land. But it's also important not to overcomplicate things. At the end of the day, the key is to put that piece of lead into a human target.

Finding a good firing position is all about getting the balance right between the maximum cover and the visual range that position affords the sniper. He needs to have a wide arc of visibility, distant enough that he avoids the main engagement of any assault or contact, but close enough to neutralise targets effectively. The further away the target, the lower the probability of a successful strike. In gentle daytime conditions, a target at a distance of less than 600m has a 70% chance of being successfully neutralised. Now, that probability reduces to 50% with the target at 600-800m and anything beyond 1,000m carries a low chance of success, although snipers can still provide harassing fire to keep enemy heads pinned down.

In addition snipers need to be able to make accurate wind calculations. It might sound unbelievable, but over a distance of 600m a round can be blown off target by a whole foot by a strong wind. This is especially true in urban environments, as towns and cities carry different wind vortexes. In natural terrain, hills can also alter the direction of the wind and influence the accuracy of the round being fired.

The mission types snipers might be asked to carry out include:

FIRE SUPPORT // The aim here is for snipers to get into firing positions prior to, or during, a main assault on a target. Coordination is vital – the snipers will look to get their rounds off simultaneously, taking out the maximum number of targets before they try to seek cover. Once the main assault begins they will locate and neutralise targets to limit the enemy's ability to confront the main assault force.

FLANK PROTECTION AND ISOLATION //

In multi-pronged attacks on the target stronghold, snipers can be used to monitor and defend the main task force's flanks against enemy attacks or counter-attacks. Using their mobility they can also take up a position to the rear of the target and isolate the enemy. Faced with a frontal assault and sniper actions to their flanks and rear, the enemy is well and truly in the shit.

OBSERVATION AND INTEL // Snipers aren't just used to take out targets. They can also be a very valuable source of intel. In a siege situation, placing snipers in surrounding buildings and getting them to train their sights on targets allows the head shed to build up a detailed picture of enemy numbers, strength, morale and movement – information that is critical to determining the success of a later assault.

SPECIAL TERRAIN MISSIONS // In certain

environments snipers can perform specialist roles that can have a critical effect on the outcome of a mission objective. In built-up urban environments such as Baghdad snipers can take advantage of the large number of firing positions available to hit the enemy hard, although the guys will avoid obvious positions that could make them vulnerable to enemy fire. In the jungle, sniper operators can carry out morale-sapping operations against guerrilla armies and provide valuable recce work from ridge lines and on rivers and waterways. In arctic terrain the guys will locate targets and maintain a stream of harassing fire, slowing enemy targets down, making them spend longer in the harsh, unforgiving cold and weakening their strength and will to fight.

COUNTERSNIPER WARFARE // This is where

snipers are used against enemy snipers. In a hostile urban environment, snipers can be an ever-present threat to friendly forces. While the accuracy of enemy snipers varies according to training, they are more than just a lethal threat – their presence drains troop morale and keeps soldiers constantly on edge and worried they will be next. Insurgents have regularly targeted US and UK soldiers in Iraq, using the densely built-up Baghdad streets to pick off unsuspecting

Operation Marlborough, which took place in July 2005 in Baghdad, is an excellent example of the effectiveness of snipers in combat situations. MI6 had received intelligence that three suicide bombers were planning to blow themselves up at busy cafes and restaurants in and around the city. The SAS decided that launching an assault on the house where the ragheads were holed up was too dangerous – if even one of the insurgents detonated the explosives strapped around their chest, all the guys would be toast. So instead they set up four Regiment snipers around the house and waited. At 8am, the suicide bombers left the house and the order was given to open fire. It was vital that the snipers not only hit their targets – but hit them in the head and killed them instantly. A round hitting them anywhere else wouldn't necessarily kill them straight away, giving the terrorists the opportunity to detonate . . .

At the signal, three of the snipers opened fire, with the fourth guy in reserve in case any of the lads had a stoppage or missed the target. The rounds .338 rounds instantly smashed through the skulls of the insurgents and their lifeless bodies flopped to the ground. None of them got the chance to detonate their violent home-made explosive bombs. As far as sniper missions go, this was a perfect execution.

servicemen. In this situation, rather than using a regular armed patrol to locate the snipers, the guys will look to bring in a friendly sniper team who will have a clear idea of the cover the enemy sniper is using, scoping out the area, gathering intel and eventually locating the enemy snipers and slotting them.

The key to effective countersniping is to gather accurate information about the enemy sniper forces. The more precise intel they have about the snipers, the better their chances of a successful take-down. Intel the guys will look to acquire will include the enemy routine (e.g. is there a particular time of day they seem to operate in), preferred firing positions, interviewing witnesses before and after the snipers have struck, the range the snipers are generally firing from and the weather conditions. Once the sniper team has assembled this information they will be able to identify where, when and how the enemy sniper team is likely to operate and prepare a counter-strike against them. In some situations the team will launch a decoy to lure the enemy snipers out – e.g. a valuable friendly target at a staged public event, with sniper teams already in place ready to take out the enemy.

Along with these specialist skills, the ability to discharge standard firearms accurately is something every soldier will need to master. A savvy, smart SF operator is ineffective unless he can fire in a straight line in a combat situation. They will also need advanced weapon training in order to be good teachers when they are dispatched to equip and lead foreign forces (as in Afghanistan in 2001). And there are also a variety of advanced skills that will be necessary for every recruit to learn: the ability to drive a number of different vehicle types, and how to make yourself inconspicuous on undercover operations.

In the United States Special Forces Groups, operators are organised into teams of 12, also known as Operational Detachment Alpha (ODA). Each soldier in an ODA is trained and cross-trained in different disciplines, listed below:

POSITION	ROLE
Special Forces Officer (Commander)	Responsible for mission organisation and debriefing mission objectives
Warrant Officer	Assistant Commander of the ODA
Weapons Sergeant	Selecting weapons and targets, studying US and foreign-manufactured weaponry

Engineering Sergeant	Experts in demolitions, navigating across land and water, sabotage and fortification
Medical Sergeant	Specialising in trauma medicine, public sanitation, dentistry, veterinary care and optometry
Communications Sergeant	Responsible for operating all comms gear, including satellite comms and Morse Code systems, as well as computer programming skills
Assistant Operations	Intel expert, gathering, evaluating and supplying mission data
Operations Sergeant	Logistics and support, makes sure the team is equipped and properly trained and prepared for the mission

CONTINUATION TRAINING SKILLS

An operator will brush up and learn several skill sets when he is deployed into an elite unit. Some of these are essential before he is allowed to undertake certain missions with the unit; others will need to be constantly practised and rehearsed during the operator's Special Forces career.

CLANDESTINE TRAINING // Originally an SAS speciality, this is also increasingly developed by other

In any SF unit, soldiers are required to learn at least TWO of the skills outlined on pages 47 and 48. If one member of the unit is killed, the rest should still be able to maintain combat effectiveness. Learning two skills or more means that the team isn't reliant on any one guy.

SF units around the world. Observation of the enemy is essential, either to build up a profile for regular armed forces' later invasion, or to call in air or artillery strikes. They say patience is a virtue and it's doubly true when performing clandestine operations. Operators need to be able to build a makeshift, well-hidden shelter from the surrounding terrain and remain on observation for extended periods of time. For example, SF operators helping to combat the violent drug cartels in Colombia would need to observe the manufacturing plants for several days without moving or being noticed, in order to gather sufficient intelligence data for a later assault.

COUNTER-TERRORIST TRAINING // In the

SAS, counter-terrorism focuses on sniper training, fast-roping and Close Quarter Battle (CQB). CQB is high-intensity stuff and was one of my favourite aspects of SAS training. Its fast and violent nature means that the guys have to be prepared for rapid engagement, at short range, against multiple targets, potentially involving unarmed combat. It is meant to replicate the terrorist situations that the SAS might have to respond to – hostage crises in civilian buildings or public transport, where space is tight and the team needs to insert and disable the terrorists as

During my time spent with Sunkar, Kazakhstan's special military police outfit, memories of CQB training came flooding back when I witnessed the team training for an assault on a passenger train occupied by 'terrorists' played by actors. I was impressed by how quickly the Sunkar lads seized control of the train, capturing the terrorists and rescuing the hostages. In CQB situations, time is of the essence.

quickly as possible – as seen most famously when the SAS ended the Iranian Embassy siege in 1980.

Counter-terrorism training also focuses on hostage rescue as many terrorist actions include the taking, and intended execution of, civilians. Sayeret Matkal, Israel's main Special Forces unit, is a specialist in hostage rescue operations beyond Israel's borders. Most famously they carried out Operation Entebbe, when they launched a daring raid on an airport building in Uganda where PLO terrorists were holding over a hundred Air France airline passengers hostage. Although one SM officer was killed during the raid, along with three hostages, the loss of life would have been much greater had SM not intervened and thwarted the PLO's plans to kill them unless their demands were met. More recently, Blades have helped to rescue hostages kidnapped by insurgents in Iraq, working in a race against time to free them before their captors chopped their heads off.

LIVE ENVIRONMENT TRAINING // Some

SF units are designed to operate in a specific geographical environment, usually in a place where there is a very rooted culture and where the team's ability to assimilate themselves amongst the people could mean the difference between life and death for a team deployed deep behind enemy lines. For some units, this is their native environment – the Kailbiles of Guatemala, for example, are trained in jungle counter-insurgency warfare. But for other units, they'll need to train and specialise in environments and terrains that are very different from their home countries.

For those SAS soldiers who progress on to Boat Troop, they will learn specialist maritime skills such as using kayaks and rigid inflatable boats (RIBS). Mountain Troop, which I was a part of, teaches its students arctic combat and survival, using specialist gear such as skis, snowshoes and mountain-climbing techniques.

When I first met up with the Junglas I was greeted by a Colonel responsible for training the lads and a former crack commander with the US Special Forces who had seen tours of duty in Panama, El Salvador and Colombia. His experience of Central and South America with the US SF makes him an ideal candidate to oversee the Junglas. Knowing the people, and the terrain and culture, means he can understand better than anyone how to motivate and discipline these eager young recruits.

The Junglas were fighting an enemy that used guerrilla tactics and operated in remote, hillside regions with heavy foliage. Their training focused on helicopter landings on dodgy slopes and under concentrated fire. It was so intense that one guy had to be medevacced after suffering a severe bullet wound to his stomach – I'm not kidding. It's as close to the real thing as you can get – and it needs to be, because nothing else can prepare them for insertion into a heavily guarded cocaine manufacturing plant.

FREEFALL TRAINING //

SAS operators will have to constantly practise freefall drills, first at RAF Brize Norton and then from a C-130 Hercules airplane with a training instructor, before they can be considered for this type of insertion. Depending on the unit, the team may also practise helicopter insertions on hostile ships and, for Boat Troop, submarine and boat insertions as well.

SPECIAL-TO-ROLE TRAINING //

covers any special role the team is required to carry out in ops. For example, the lads in the US Special Forces are expected to train and organise insurgents, guerrilla fighters, native forces and foreign armies. Training is an integral part of SF operations in the modern world, and if the unit is able to effectively teach irregulars how to fight and win battles, that can have a huge influence on the outcome of a military conflict.

In the build-up to the Iraq War, the US 10th Special Forces Group was inserted into Northern Iraq prior to the main invasion. There they contacted, organised and trained Kurdish separatist forces. During the war, these joint Kurdish-Special Forces units defeated several Iraqi Army Divisions, with no operators killed and eliminating more than a thousand enemy combatants. Such a successful Northern invasion would not have been possible had the 10th SFG not been well-trained in teaching the dark arts of war to the Kurds.

Guerrilla warfare training isn't just useful for training indigenous forces – it's also important when the SF team is inserting into an environment that is occupied by guerrilla forces. The hit-and-run attacks of guerrillas require a different mindset, approach and solution to regular enemy combatants.

Guerrilla armies are difficult to plan for as the skill of their soldiers can vary greatly. You can encounter guerrillas who fire their Kalashnikovs from the hip Rambo-style and can't aim for chips, like the gangs that Delta Force faced on Operation Gothic Serpent in Somalia. Then there are some guerrilla armies that are excellently trained in weaponry and warfare despite the lack of government backing – the Tamil Tigers in Sri Lanka are well organised and lethal in combat situations, and the al-Qaeda fighters in Afghanistan have become sharp shooters after years of practise in warfare. I've heard from mates fighting out there of the improved accuracy of the enemy – one guy even saw enemy rounds striking against the ammo on his belt-fed heavy machine gun, the shots were *that* close. That accuracy has come as a bit of a surprise to operators used to the 'Pray and Spray' tactics of Iraqi insurgents.

Other units might need to specialise in surveillance and carry out a lot of recces to brush up their observational skills. Typically, special-to-role training can take around 12 to 14 months.

CROSS-TRAINING // The SAS might be the world's finest soldiers, but the reason they are so successful is because they are constantly looking to improve. There is no better way to do this than to train with elite units from other countries. It's a great chance to compare fighting techniques and learn survival secrets from operators who have perhaps had more combat experience in a different environment. Units like the SAS, Delta Force, German Grenschutzgruppe-9 (GSG 9) and Australian SAS Regiment cross-train on a regular basis. This often involves competitions between the units. There's nothing like a bit of friendly rivalry to keep the guys razor sharp.

The amount of gear a soldier carries has to strike a delicate balance between mobility and protection. For that reason the equipment an operator is kitted out in varies from mission to mission, but in today's operations elite units tend to be stripped down to the bare basics. This is very different from regular servicemen, who are arguably weighed down with too much gear – body armour (nicknamed 'Plate Hangers' after the ceramic plate that slips inside the armour front and back), knee and elbow pads and state-of-the-art helmets are all good and proper, but it can severely dent a soldier's mobility in the furnace-like temperatures of Afghanistan and Iraq.

EQUIPMENT AND WEAPONS

SPECIALIST EQUIPMENT

For a Special Forces soldier, having the proper gear can mean the difference between life and death. Whatever the mission, any elite unit needs a lot of equipment to carry out the operation successfully.

Some bits of kit are specific to different environments – of course, skis, snowshoes and ice-picks aren't much use in the sweltering jungles of Central America, while a hammock, mozzie net and malaria drugs are not ideal tools for an Arctic tab. But there's a bunch of stuff that's absolute must-have, wherever the team is being dropped into.

CAMOUFLAGE FATIGUES // Camo comes in different types. The most recognisable is the sand, green, brown and black combo used in woodlands and wetlands combat, known as Disruptive Pattern Material (DPM). Then there's 'chocolate-chip' camo, used by US SF in desert terrain, made up of tan, olive green and browns. Finally, digital camo (known as 'dual-tex') uses smaller micropatterns than the larger ones used on DPM, the idea being that smaller patterns are harder to detect to the human eye. Digi-cam was introduced in the Eighties and is now used by the Marine Corps, as well as several other units around the world.

Natural camo should always be taken from the surrounding terrain – for example, using natural foliage to cover the helmet and head. This is a good way of making sure the operator blends into the immediate environment. Tying it together with hessian material ensures that there's no obvious white string or tape that compromises the camo effect.

In the SAS it used to be the case that we all had to wear the same uniform, right down to the same windproof smocks. Today however it's pretty much a case of wear what you want, whatever's comfortable and works best.

RESPIRATORS // When the mission involves CQB, stun grenades are often used to disorientate potential threats before the soldiers enter the room or confined space. The blinding flash and deafening bang of the G60 stun grenade used by Special Forces gives the unit a precious few seconds' advantage when clearing a room, but can only be done when accompanied by a gas mask or respirator, to protect the operator's eyes and ears. Respirators can also be used in infiltration missions when there is a genuine nuclear, biological or chemical (NBC) threat – in the Gulf War soldiers were given the S10 NBC Respirator to protect against possible Scud chemical warheads.

BALLISTIC SHIELDS // These are armoured shields that are capable of stopping a 7.62mm round and provide invaluable protection for entry teams in CQB situations. The guy holding the ballistic shield will grip onto it using a handle. The shield covers most of the holder's frame so operators generally follow behind the shield bearer in a stack formation, delivering fire from behind the shield wearer, with the shield dramatically reducing the effective target area.

NBC (NUCLEAR, BIOLOGICAL, CHEMICAL) SUIT // Are carried when operators are undertaking missions in environments where the enemy is believed to have access to 'dirty' weaponry such as chemical warheads. These are designed to be fitted easily and quickly over the operator's standard clothing.

The days of old-fashioned radios are long gone for Special Forces. Nowadays most outfits use **iridium satellite phones** to maintain contact with other assault or reconnaissance elements and the head shed. In the Regiment we also used **TACBE**s (Tactical

Beacons) to contact overhead aircraft or helicopters. The TACBE sends out a distress signal and means the team is in danger or needs help (such as a medevac or emergency exfiltration).

The frequencies available are HF (High Frequency), VHF (Very High Frequency), UHF (Ultra High Frequency) and SHF (Super High Frequency). Encryption devices are also used. In recent years, SHF SATCOM has been the band frequency most used by Special Forces operations, with UHF SATCOM being used for voice and data traffic. Advances in technology mean that these frequencies can be built into a single multi-purpose radio such as the American JASORS (Joint Advanced Special Operations Radio System) device.

Personal Role Radio (PRR) headsets, strapped to the operator's head, are light – just 1.5kg – and have a range of 500m in open terrain, allowing units to stay in contact over substantial distances. The headsets are also operational through three separate floors in a building, and can travel through solid walls.

In E&E situations, radio communications might be intercepted, and operators now generally use a variant GPS tracking system as well, called the

Combat Survivor/Evader Locator (CSEL). GPS units are an invaluable addition to SF teams operating in the desert or Arctic. Over-the-horizon satellites send time-coded signals down to the GPS units, and these signals are used to triangulate the GPS unit's position. In the Gulf War, our patrol was given Magellan GPS units to help us navigate through the often flat, featureless Iraqi plains.

LASER TARGET DESIGNATORS (LTDS) //

These portable devices establish targets for friendly aircraft to pulverise into oblivion. LTDs are tripod-mounted and have an optical sight, range finder and a laser emitter. The laser is shone at the target. Once the target is 'painted', the laser bounces off the target and is transmitted to a sensor on board the aircraft. A laser-guided bomb or missile is then launched and locks in on the laser. This is a crafty bit of gear and a far less risky way to blow up key targets rather than steaming in guns blazing or planting explosives.

BODY ARMOUR //
The mantra amongst the world's elite forces today is 'keep it as light as possible', but on CQB missions or urban ops where the risk of close-range gunfire or knife attacks is much higher, Kevlar body armour is reasonably light and

can be tucked away underneath a disguise. Knee, elbow and shoulder pads might also be worn to protect the wearer when breaking through a smashed window or using grenades or shotguns in a compact environment.

NIGHT VISION GOGGLES (NVGS) // Light enough to be mounted on a helmet or even on a pair of binoculars, the latest generation of units come with image intensifier tubes as well as thermal image processing, are water-resistant, and often include telescopic lenses too, giving the guys a unique advantage in night-time combat.

BASIC KIT

A *compass* and *map* might seem old-fashioned compared to all the hi-tech GPS gear, but they're vital all the same. You never know when technology systems could go wrong and break down. In emergency situations, an operator has to be able to navigate using the most basic tools available.

BERGEN/BACKPACK // As used by all British Special Forces. Comes in the same camo style as the rest of the soldier's clothing. As a general rule operators should not carry more than 50% of their body weight, which equates to a maximum recommended marching load of around 100lb for an elite operator. You can attach side pouches for extra load bearing. Some SF outfits now use backpacks fitted with hydration systems instead. The special design of these systems increases the amount of water the soldier can carry, making it ideal for longer tabs or ops in environments where water intake is crucial, such as jungle or desert missions. They come fitted with drinking tubes that feed directly from the backpack to the operator's mouth, meaning he can rehydrate himself while he's on the move.

When I was in Mountain Troop, during Arctic operations we would use the Arctic Bergen. The Arctic Bergen fits higher up on the operator's back, creating less drag on his core – ideal when he needs to ski.

SOCKS AND BOOTS // One of the first things you're taught as a Blade is to take good care of your feet. They're your number one mode of mobility and if your feet are knackered you can't do patrols, which are the bread and butter of Special Forces ops. I'm a great believer in the effective, sturdy, standard-issue Army boots. They now come in a model that is cut a bit lower, making it easier to put on and remove. They're reliable, solid and get the job done. Other elite operators can be a bit fussy and fork out for their own boots. There's a wide range of Gore-Tex boots available, made of a breathable synthetic that allows sweat to get out but prevents water from getting in. Other boots are used for special types of ops: quick-drying Cambrelle types are ideal for patrols through damp terrain, and reinforced boots with greater grip and built-in shock absorption might be worn on house-clearances and urban warfare. Berghaus mountain boots can be attached to skis and snowshoes. Gore-Tex socks are also worn by SF guys.

Sleeping bags and **mats** and **waterproofs** help keep operators dry and warm.

Elite operators tend to avoid wearing **helmets** on deep surveillance missions. For CQB missions in compact environments like hotels or airplanes they will wear an armoured or ceramic helmet for extra protection, which can withstand the force of a 9mm round at close range. In the desert, Blades will still wear a shemagh to protect the head and neck from the sun.

Each team member will have some generic **medical kit**, such as field dressings to reduce blood loss. In addition the team's specialist medic will have some painkillers, an inflatable splint to temporarily fix broken limbs, plasma-expanders (to stabilise casualties who experience severe blood loss resulting from gut wounds or severed joints), and antibiotic creams and capsules. The medic will also carry some surgical tools and dentistry equipment for field jobs, as well as the obligatory morphine to ease the pain in battlefield emergencies.

You'll never find the lads raving about the quality of **rations**, but the fact is that 21st-century ration packs are light years ahead of the bad old days of canned goods like beef and peas that weighed a ton and tasted awful. The amount of calories an operator burned lugging the ration packs round was more than he got from eating them!

In the Regiment we stick to boil-in-the-bags. The main entrees come in sealed polythene bags for extra protection and can be submerged in water then heated up, although the meals have been pre-cooked so you can eat them cold too – useful as there are very few opportunities during a patrol when an operator will have the chance to warm it up. The soups and drinks are powdered or instant. You can heat up the boil-in-the-bag entrees on a small hexamine stove (also called a Tommy cooker). This

When I was in the Regiment, we'd stock up on Mars Bars or Kendal mint cake. It's vital to load up on calories when you're on operations, and these provide a sugary, energy-releasing supplement to whatever 'main meals' we had. Energy and protein bars are also good 'grazing' foods.

uses blocks of hexamine for fuel – the blocks are toxic and can be difficult to light because they are so waxy. But the stove is very portable and handy, and can be used to heat up water for a brew as well.

Each ration pack provides the soldier with around 4,000 calories a day – but if he's pulling a sixty-kilometre tab he's still going to be operating with a negative calorie intake. For that reason, SF teams can survive on ration packs for a maximum of between 15-30 days, depending on the terrain and the nature of the mission, without suffering any serious nutritional side effects. Thirty days is the absolute limit though. As a general rule, most operations will last less than that – two weeks at most. Special Forces rely on mobility and stealth – if the mission lasts any longer, the soldiers risk being weighed down by physical and mental fatigue.

WEAPONS

When I first signed up for service, I was the same as the other lads – I couldn't wait to get out on the firing range and let rip. Time and experience changes your perspective, and I soon understood just how deadly guns were, especially in the wrong hands. For SF units,

I would say that biggest is not always best. With soldiers having to carry over 100lb of equipment, there's absolutely no point in operators on a jungle patrol lugging round heavy machine guns that will slow them down and could also develop faults in the damp, wet jungle environment. The weapons an SF soldier carries should also be suited to a variety of challenging combat environments, because a mission deep behind enemy lines could require rifles for long-range combat as well as semi-automatics or pistols for close-quarters firefights. As ever, getting the balance right, to reflect the mission plan, is vital.

There are seven basic categories of weapons that special ops guys use:

ANTI-ARMOUR WEAPONS // As the name suggests, these are designed to destroy vehicles and equipment. Of limited use in the field and often bulky to carry.

GRENADE LAUNCHERS // Along with anti-armour weapons, the Regiment also refers to these as 'force multipliers' – defined as something that allows a small force to be combat-effective against a much larger one. Whether standalone or as mounted underslung onto an assault rifle, these are brilliant at causing a wide field of damage. They're like mortars, but without the hassle of having to set one up.

MACHINE GUNS // come in heavy, medium or light sizes. Heavy machine guns pack a serious punch and with a plus-.50 calibre bore can take out light vehicles, but they're a big additional weight for an operator to take. Medium guns such as minimis and light guns like GMPGs (also known as Gimpys) are good at firing bursts and are more mobile weapons, and hence more suited to longer tabs and on-foot deployments.

SHOTGUNS // good for close-range combat and suited to counter-terrorism warfare such as CQB.

SUB-MACHINE GUNS // Short and compact, these are not the most accurate of weapons, but they make up for this through their usefulness as silent killers – because of the low power of the cartridge in sub-machine guns, they are very well suited to suppression and a variety of add-on suppressors make SMGs an option when considering weaponry for covert operations.

RIFLES // come in several types. Sniper rifles offer precision accuracy over distances from 300-2,300m depending on the cartridge size. A 5.56 × 45mm round is effective up to 500m, whereas a 14.5 × 114mm cartridge can take out a target at a distance of 2,300m. The longer range cartridges mean snipers can fire from further away, meaning they have to take less risks when it comes to concealment. Multi-purpose rifles, while not as accurate as the sniper type, are still good long-range weapons but can also be used for short-range actions such as ambushes and CQB, where the target is right on top of the operator.

HANDGUNS // Regular armed forces tend to ignore the handgun, but for SF teams, secondary weapons can be very useful. Although the primary weapons an SF team chooses are usually very reliable, there are times when they suffer a stoppage (as happened to a guy I was training with during an exercise with the Magav, Israel's border police), or are lost or abandoned along with other carried equipment during an E&E exercise. In these cases, the operator has to fall back on his handgun, which is the only weapon lightweight enough to be carried on his escape belt.

The choice of weapon an operator will use boils down to what type of mission he is facing. For house clearances and close protection you would use the MP5 for its compact but effective features. Rifles are better suited to conventional warfare such as Iraq and Afghanistan, where guns with greater accuracy and range are necessary. Heavy, medium and light machine guns form part of a patrol's support weapons for taking on larger forces, again in conventional warfare situations. Pistols, as a secondary weapon, are useful in nearly every combat scenario.

Some of my favourite weapons are:

M4 COLT COMMANDO // The weapon of choice for Blades. Light, with a choice of three settings – single-shot, semi-automatic and three-round burst – this is a great rifle for close-combat and urban warfare. It's more convenient to carry than a regular-size and weight assault rifle, and a lot of SF teams use it on a frequent basis, such as US Army Special Forces and Navy SEALs. Recently I got the chance to get reacquainted with this old friend when working alongside the feared BOPE (*Batalhão de Operações Policiais Especiais*, or *Special Police Operations Battalion*) elite police force In Rio de Janeiro.

The lads in the Regiment use what used to be called a Diemaco C8, a Canadian-manufactured weapon that looks a lot like the Colt Commando on the outside, but has slightly different internals machinery. Diemaco was bought out by Colt but everyone in the trade still calls it a Diemaco.

HECKLER AND KOCH MP5 // The ultimate sub-machine gun, this is the standard weapon for the SAS in CQB. It's fearsome. Because the MP5 is so popular, there are now literally hundreds of variants of it on the market, but my personal favourite is the MP5A2; it takes a 9×19mm Parabellum cartridge and has a fluted chamber that bleeds gases back down the flutes to prevent the cartridge case from expanding as it flies down the chamber. It also has adjustable iron sights, making it easy to pinpoint targets, and comes in a suppressed version too (the MP5SD). Take it from me, this is a really great gun, with a range of 25m to 100m. Comes in single-shot, semi-automatic and automatic variations, along with the choice of two- or three-shot bursts. The MP5 is particularly good for CQB and ideal for hostage-rescue operations because the 9mm round is unlikely to pass through the target or walls and injure a hostage, and the suppressor means that enemy targets can be taken down without alerting nearby forces.

ACCURACY INTERNATIONAL L96 // This bolt-action sniper rifle is used across all the Armed Forces and it has a reputation as a reliable, effective and durable weapon ideal for sniper operations. First introduced in the 1980s, the L96 has a first-round range of 600m and is capable of putting down suppressive fire up to 1,100m. It uses a 7.62mm round and comes in single shot format and can be fitted with a bipod to provide extra stability during combat. It also features a × 3, × 12 and × 50 sight. Gradually this has been replaced by the **L115A3 Long Range Rifle** which is chambered with 8.599mm rounds that are less likely to be deflected off course over long ranges. The L115A3 comes with Harris bipod legs and a 5-25 × 56 telescopic day scope that allows the operator to engage targets at distances up to 1,200m away. The L115A3 can also be used in night-time operations thanks to a SIMRAD KN203D sight. Night-time hits are less successful than daytime ops, with target kill probability reduced to 30% across all distances regardless of rifle type. There are variations on the Accuracy range such as the covert **AWS (Arctic Warfare Suppressed)** edition which can be broken down into components for undercover operations.

MII SIG SAUER P228 9MM // the standard pistol. Small, light (weighing just 1.10lb) famously durable, it's as dependable a handgun as there's ever been.

BROWNING HI-POWER // a bit of a nostalgic choice as this was the first pistol I used as a young soldier. The Browning is the classic 9mm handgun. Although it's old in firearms terms, dating back to before the Second World War, the Browning is still a popular handgun because it is very easily maintained.

L2A2 HAND GRENADE // A high-explosive anti-personnel grenade, this is one of the best in the market, packed with 170g of RDX/TNT, with a 4.4 second delay and lethal radius of 10m. Grenades are an effective way of causing sustained damage to pinned-down enemy targets hiding behind protection, such as a car or behind a wall. With practice of the various throwing techniques, elite operators can use grenades to neutralise the enemy in a wide variety of combat situations.

In addition to their own weapons, Special Forces troopers will also get to grips with many of the world's most commonly used military weapons manufactured in China or Eastern Europe, such as the **AK-47**. More commonly known as the **Kalashnikov**, the AK-47 is used by millions of regular and irregular armed forces around the world. The reason it's so popular is because, as weapons go, it's virtually indestructible and unstoppable. You can freeze it, burn it or bury it, and it'll still work every time. Reliability, plus a simple design that means the gun can be manufactured around the world easily and cheaply, makes the AK-47 the weapon of choice for guerrilla armies, terrorist cells and insurgents across the globe. In Africa you can pick up an AK-47 for as little as $20. It also packs a serious punch and is ideal for short-range warfare. In fact, the AK-47 was so dependable that until recently the carbine edition, the AKSU, was the weapon of choice for Spetsnaz units, although it is being slowly phased out and replaced by the new AN-94 Abakan assault rifle.

Given that so many regular and irregular forces use the AK-47, it pays for an elite operator to have intimate knowledge of this type of weapon. Not only might they be tasked with training foreign militaries with their use, they may also lead such forces into combat, using indigenously sourced firearms depending on the operation logistics. Knowing foreign firearms is also vital knowledge for escape and evasion scenarios, where SF teams will need to use any weapons they can get their hands on. Sometimes, in order to breach security undetected, operators will disguise themselves as the enemy, mimicking the dress codes (even down to using worry beads in Islamic countries) and carrying the same weapons as local gangs and militias. This procedure is known as going 'false flag'.

The different operating roles of Special Forces units require a multitude of weapons, to suit the terrain and enemy they are trained to fight. Some of the other weapons used by Western Special Forces outfits include:

M4A1 CARBINE // a high-tech, multi-purpose assault rifle. The M4A1 is a supremely adaptable beast, and with the use of optics and lasers can be used effectively in night-time operations. Excellent for counter-terrorism ops, its other key advantage is that it's bang on the money as both an accurate weapon and a versatile carbine. It's light and comfortable enough to carry on special ops and in airborne insertions as it takes up less space. Its 5.6mm rounds can penetrate body armour.

HECKLER AND KOCH MARK 23 // A semi-automatic with a laser guide attached, and can be used with a suppressor too. It weighs 1.2 kg when empty, going up to 2.3 kg when loaded with suppressor, laser attachment and ammo. Both waterproof and anti-corrosive, it is extremely durable and can survive almost constant use in unforgiving environments, making it ideal for long-range SF patrols. It uses .45 ACP ammo, and for those who need something a little smaller, also comes in a pocket-friendly version called the USP Tactical.

BENELLI M4 SUPER 90 / REMINGTON SHOTGUN // Traditionally these were used in jungle ops as a lead scout weapon because of the spread of the shot, until they were superseded by the M16, which has a fully automatic mode. They are back in vogue now in Iraq and Afghanistan as a method of entry weapon in house clearances.

LAW 66 ROCKET LAUNCHER // A single-shot, disposable launcher that fires a 66mm unguided pre-loaded rocket projectile with an explosive head. Highly effective against light vehicles, and with an effective range of between 200 and 1,000m, this is a very mobile and easy to use weapon. When I was training with Israel's Magav, I got the chance to use this weapon again.

GLOCK 9MM // As used by the Regiment, and by many elite paramilitary and police units around the world. Light and easy to carry in a holster on your leg during operations, the Glock uses 9×19mm parabellum cartridges. There are many versions of

the Glock available on the market to suit different operational needs.

Of course, not all Special Forces use the same set of guns. The type of unit, the environment they operate in and even the gun-manufacturing tradition in their country, can all influence the weapon selection available to a unit. During my time working with elite paramilitary units around the world I was reminded about how each unit employs a whole array of weapons that I didn't get a chance to use when I was a Blade.

PECHENEG HEAVY MACHINE GUN // I got the chance to use this with the Sunkar in Kazakhstan. Firing a 7.63 × 54mm round and featuring a handle over the barrel that keeps it cool, the Pecheneg was developed in the wake of the Soviet Union's chastening experience in Afghanistan. Heavy machine guns are famous for lacking pinpoint accuracy, but the Pecheneg is the exception to the rule. As well as impressive accuracy, the Pecheneg doesn't have much of a kick to it, making it surprisingly stable. Great weapon.

SAKO TRG-22 SNIPER RIFLE // This Finnish-designed sniper rifle was used during BOA's training exercise bus assault. Using .308 Winchester rounds

Above: The SAS are the original and the best special forces outfit in the world. Many of their standard operating procedures were learnt during hard grafts in treacherous environments, such as the jungles of Malaya in the 1950s.

A US Special Forces operator in camouflage and with a single night sight. A lot of SF missions take place at night, and the elite operator has to be an expert In conducting nocturnal warfare operations.

A BOA operator adopts the kneeling firing position, ready to engage the enemy.

Lying down provides maximum cover. The mag is taped on so it doesn't fall apart, as older magazines can split and spill out rounds.

Getting to grips with foreign weapons such as the AK-47 is a vital skill for all elite operators.

Spetsnaz soldiers during arctic warfare training. Different elite units need to focus on specialist combat and survival skills, depending on the environment they are trained to fight in.

Above: Sunkar are Kazakhstan's elite paramilitary unit. Their weapons systems originate from Eastern Europe.

Below: Mexico's Policia Federal Assault Group are specially trained in riot and urban warfare and equipped accordingly – note the Black Hawk in the background. They use female officers in riot situations (left) to disable female rioters thus avoiding unwanted bad press.

Left: Body armour is a double-edged sword – it weighs operators down and reduces their mobility, but can prove a lifesaver. The armour I'm wearing here has studs to slap extra pouches onto.

Below: The ballistic shield as used by Mexico's Policia Federal. This shield can absorb a 7.62mm round and offers great protection to the team. The guy second from right at the front is using a paintball gun in training to see if he can hit the target accurately in a frantic close-range firefight.

Above: Handguns such as the Beretta 9mm are good secondary weapons. They only need one hand to hold rather than two, so are also good when detaining suspects in hostage rescue scenarios.

Below: The stripped down Heckler & Koch MP5 and, right, the same weapon as used by a BOA operator, fitted with torch, sight and double magazine clipped to the side to reduce the time spent loading a new magazine – rather than reaching down into his pouch, the operator already has the next magazine to hand, ready to load.

Above: The Colt Commando in action. It's the staple weapon of elite outfits around the world and a weapon I've used for many years.

Above: The Sig-Sauer P288 9mm is a highly resilient secondary weapon.

Left: Test-firing the Browning 9mm.

Grenades are great at reaching targets that are hiding behind protection such as cars or walls, with a kill zone of 5m and an effective range of 15m. They should be thrown in an overarm motion similar to bowling a cricket ball, not underarm, in order to achieve the maximum possible flight and accuracy. Just make sure you duck after throwing it, otherwise you might get shrapnel in your face!

this is a precision rifle designed specially for sniper ops. With a telescopic sight and effective up to 800m, the Sako can also be fitted with a muzzle brake that reduces weapon recoil and kickback, meaning the sniper can move quickly from one target to the next. A suppressor can also be fitted for operations where silent sniping is required.

GM-94 GRENADE LAUNCHER // Fires

thermobaric plastic grenades. Thermobaric weapons are ones that use atmospheric oxygen to initiate the explosion, rather than an oxidiser in the round itself. This creates more explosive energy, producing a wider killing field. Put it this way, anyone caught in the vicinity of a thermobaric round is going to the dark side. The GM-94 can also fire tear-gas shells when suppression rather than destruction is the objective. It has a kill radius of 3 metres, and can be safely used during room-to-room searches, without the operator risking hitting himself or his teammates with frag.

During my time with the Sunkar in Kazakhstan, I got the chance to become acquainted with the GM-94 for the first time. I'd heard about this weapon during my time with the SAS, and the thrill of using what had been an enemy weapon just a few years' previously, was only matched by its hugely impressive capability.

The rounds are powerful enough to take out a light armoured vehicle, and it packs a meaty punch. Take it from me, this is one hell of a weapon.

RPG-7 // The RPG-7 anti-tank grenade launcher was developed by the Soviets in the early 1960s and was the Commies' answer to the M72 LAW. Durable, simple to use and packing a serious punch, the RPG has become notorious in recent years as terrorist groups from every field of combat from Somalia to Chechnya and Iraq have adopted it, but Spetsnaz military units still use it in combat operations. Shoulder-fired, muzzle-loaded, this launches fin-stabilised grenades from a 40mm tube. Effective up to 300m, the RPG-7 can take out firing positions and although it can't destroy a tank by itself, two or three RPGs fired simultaneously at a target is enough to put it out of commission. The RPG-7 is so reliable that, during the Soviet-Afghanistan war, Spetsnaz soldiers issued with the much less effective RPG-16 or 22 types would take the 7 model from captured Mujahideen. Nowadays the RPG-7 is more famous for taking down Western helicopters, but as a weapon for elite operators, it takes some beating.

In counter-terrorist situations, operators will have access to further non-lethal weapons that can be used

Being skilled with weapons is more than about being able to hit the target. It's also about using the right guns for the right job, and using weapons in a coordinated, controlled way, achieving maximum suppression with minimum rounds fired. During my time with the world's elite police units, I found that the guys in BOA, Poland's special police force, had some of the best gun skills I've seen outside the Regiment.

to destabilise the enemy. Specialist stun devices are used, such as the 'Flashbang' G60. When detonated this produces a 160-decibel bang. That's incredibly loud – a jet taking off produces a 130-decibel level sound. The G60 also emits a blindingly bright flash and the dual effect is to create temporary sensory confusion of the target, reducing their combat effectiveness. The average stun effect lasts for 3-5 seconds. There is also the **CS Grenade** which contains 53g of CS gas, enveloping the immediate area in CS once detonated. The British-designed **Arwen 37 Launcher** is an excellent weapon that fires 37mm projectiles, and can be used in CQB missions to launch tear gas canisters into a confined space prior to a forward entry assault on a building or room.

As well as guns, SF soldiers will carry **knives**. As the very last line of defence in warfare, traditional combat knives are popular in a lot of SF units, especially the Commando Dagger made by Fairbairn-Sykes. Jungle knives are an essential part of any operator's kit. In the Regiment the knife of preference is a hunting knife. Some guys use a Parang knife, a Malaya equivalent of the machete which is great as a survival knife. On the other hand, the Americans prefer the specialised Kukris from Nepal. The Gurkhas also use this bad boy, which is a seriously heavy duty curved

Just as with guns, so operators need to be trained in the proper application and use of knives. The Parang tends to spring a lot when it's struck against hardwood, for example. During a training exercise in the jungle with the Regiment, I saw one instructor show his students how to strike a Parang. The guy swung it against a tree stump, and the blade swung violently back and cut him across the leg. Pretending to ignore his cock-up, he continued to lecture the students as his trousers slowly turned dark red. Then, at the end of the lecture, he suddenly fell back and collapsed from massive blood loss!

blade. With a rubberised grip, powdercoated, stainless steel blade 10 inches long and 3/16 inches thick, this is a top-class weapon of war.

Swiss army knives have been in use by SF around the world for decades. The Regiment uses the Leatherman knives, tools that have everything from screwdrivers, files, pliers, blades and saws as attachments, all crafted from stainless steel and useful in almost any environment.

Other kit that's standard to most SF outfits is binoculars, night vision scopes, extra rounds of ammunition, torches, string or twine, and plastic bags to store human waste and rubbish (excrement and Mars Bars wrappers are dead giveaways of recent human activity for trackers).

All told, I spent eleven years in the Regiment and saw action in Iraq, Sierra Leone and Zaire. Those were, and still are, some of the most brutal and oppressive places on earth, and where violence is part of daily life. And I know that if it wasn't for my training and equipment, I would never have made it out alive from any of those environments. I owe my life to my Special Forces training – as does every soldier, at some point or another, in any SF unit around the world. And that's why I put this section at the front of this book. Because everything I've talked about in this section is vital to the success or failure of a Special Forces mission. From basic training right the way through to providing for scenarios where the best-laid plans go wrong, if the mission preparation stage is done properly and no corners are cut or scenarios ignored, that gives the team the best chance of successfully completing the operation and minimising casualties. If the mission stage is badly prepared for, the chance of success is greatly reduced. I can't stress enough how important elite training is.

**Inserting into a war zone
requires training, speed,
intelligence and luck.
But most of all, it needs
stealth.**

03 GOING IN BY AIR

> **ONCE THE MISSION OBJECTIVE HAS BEEN ESTABLISHED, THE TEAM MUST PREPARE FOR INSERTION //**

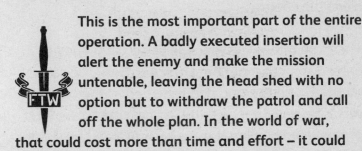

This is the most important part of the entire operation. A badly executed insertion will alert the enemy and make the mission untenable, leaving the head shed with no option but to withdraw the patrol and call off the whole plan. In the world of war, that could cost more than time and effort – it could cost lives.

The aim of Special Forces is therefore to get into the combat environment with the minimum of fuss – and without attracting the enemy's attention.

This is easier said than done. Insertion into any combat zone, whether it's an embassy under siege, or a country the operator's government is at war with, is riddled with dangers. It's a race against time to get in there fast enough that you don't give the enemy time to pinpoint your location and launch a counter-attack. When I was in the Regiment, dropping into a combat zone as quickly and efficiently as possible was a key part of our training. We even invented the famous 'tree jumping' technique (I'll talk about that a bit later in the Air section). The number one rule is: A covert mission is compromised if the insertion alerts the enemy.

There are three ways for any Special Forces unit to enter a combat zone: **Air**, **Land** and **Sea**. The tactics, methods of entry, and dangers of each approach are very different. But one thing remains the same: 90% of the time, avoiding the enemy is better than slotting him. This is the one part of the mission where you *don't* want to make a big bang.

AIRBORNE

Airborne insertion is possible in one of two ways: parachuting from an airplane, or being dropped in by helicopter. As helicoptering in is the preferred method of insertion for Special Forces today, I'll talk about that first.

HELICOPTER INSERTION AND EXTRACTION

In today's world, elite operators are most likely to insert into enemy territory by helicopter. Ever since the days of Vietnam, when helicopters became an integral part of US military operations, they have become increasingly central to elite operations.

Helicopter air assault missions require specific planning and training if they are to be executed properly.

HELICOPTER LANDING ZONES

When inserting troops by helicopter, the same basic considerations as airplane landings have to be taken into account, i.e. making sure the landing site is clear of obstacles and debris. However, they will also need to take into account the wind direction, as helicopters usually land into the wind – crosswinds or extreme winds make it difficult for helicopters to land. And sometimes the team Pathfinders will not have the time to clear the LZ of all debris, or obstacles are too big to be removed manually (i.e. rocks). In these cases, the guys will debus by either abseiling (rappelling) or fast-roping.

FAST-ROPING // is a technique that was developed to provide a reliable and quick method of deploying a group of elite operators into virtually any environment, whether the top of a building that needs to be assaulted, or into a combat zone where the team needs to carry out an urgent search and rescue mission. The technique involves grasping a thick, non-rotating synthetic rope, around 44mm in thickness, and sliding down it from the helicopter, wearing thick gloves so you don't burn your hands to bloody shreds.

When the helicopter comes to a hovering stop over the target LZ, the first fast roper will begin his descent. Placing his hands on the opposite side of the rope, palms facing in, with the stronger hand higher than the weaker one, the operator will lock his elbows out in the bracing position and slide down the rope. If he needs to slow his descent he will 'Chinese burn' the rope, twisting his hands in opposite directions. Whether or not he needs to break, he will also round his back and look down the rope, focusing on the distance to the LZ. Once he hits the turf he will move away quickly from the rope, so that he doesn't collide with the second guy down. This also gives him a chance to survey the surrounding area.

The SAS invented the fast-roping technique and it's now practised by Special Forces units all around the world. I used fast-rope techniques frequently during my time in the Regiment, and recently I got to fast-rope again on a training exercise with BOA, Poland's elite police force. It's a brilliantly effective but high-risk method for inserting into combat zones. It definitely gets the adrenaline pumping.

The maximum height for fast-roping is 60ft, and three operators can descend the rope at a time. Fast-roping, like the name suggests, is speedier than rappelling but more dangerous, so the guys have to keep a close eye on their load. If the load is too heavy then the operator could crash to the ground and severely injure himself. Fast-roping is another reason why helicopter insertion is so effective in today's war zones.

ABSEILING OR RAPPELLING // This is where the operator is connected using a figure-eight descender on a Marlow rope and is better suited to inserting into jungle environments. If you fast-roped into the jungle you'd get caught on branches because you can't control your descent. But with rappelling you're able to lock the figure-eight descender, suspend your descent, clear any obstacles, and then continue sliding down. The drawback to rappelling is that if the operator does get caught up in canopy or foliage, the team on-board the helicopter will cut him loose – otherwise the helicopter would get weighed down by the operator and crash. Rappelling is also commonly used for going down lift shafts in high-rise buildings and the sides of buildings.

Rappelling from a helicopter is possible from a variety of aircraft, including the Chinook, Sea King, Lynx and

When rappelling down the sides of buildings elite operators use exactly the same techniques as mountaineering. With your feet shoulder-width apart, make sure that you're at a 90° angle to the building and put your trust in the rope – don't try and cling on to the building.

Wessex models. Rappelling is not as rapid for entry as fast-roping, but it does offer a more controlled descent, for insertion of smaller groups with heavier personal loads, and from a greater height – up to 180ft.

The US Army Special Forces are aided by the 160th Special Operations Aviation Regiment – commonly called the 'Nightstalkers'. These guys provide aviation support to SF teams and specialise in inserting troopers into hostile environments. They use state-of-the-art helicopters, modified for their special needs, to carry out their missions.

TYPES OF HELICOPTER

MH-60 BLACK HAWK // Made famous by the movie *Black Hawk Down* which was based on the ill-fated Operation Gothic Serpent in Mogadishu, Somalia, the Black Hawk is great for tactical transport, electronic warfare in advance of an insertion and medevacs. But it's more than a transport helicopter. It's also an attack aircraft that can be armed to the teeth. Black Hawks can be fitted with 7.62mm miniguns, 70mm rocket pods, .50-calibre machine guns, 30mm canons, Stinger air-to-air missiles and Hellfire air-to-ground missiles, making it one serious war machine capable of causing massive devastation to enemy forces on the ground. This is especially useful in locations where the SF team is in E&E mode and is being chased by a heavily armed enemy force. The Black Hawk can pulverise the force and then evacuate the team to safety.

MH-6 LITTLE BIRD //

Heavy duty Blackhawks are all well and good, but for missions that require the rapid insertion or extraction of SF teams into narrow, obstacle-filled areas, the Little Bird, with a maximum speed of 152 knots (175mph, 282km/h) is perfect. Virtually undetectable due to its small size, it has benches fitted on either side to ferry up to six troopers, and is painted black for concealment during night-time operations. A modified version, the AH-6, is an attack helicopter that can carry much of the same arsenal as the Black Hawk, and also comes fitted with an ALQ-144 infra-red jammer and radar warning receiver.

MH-47D CHINOOK //

Powered by two turbo-shaft engines, the Chinook is capable of lifting medium to heavy loads and is ideal for transporting SF units across long distances to the LZ – and quickly too, averaging a top speed of 170 knots (196mph). For extractions, the Chinook comes with a rescue hoist,

Little Birds can be used as weapons platforms, and can literally fly down a street at the same level as a car – they have the same capabilities as an F1 car and are able to turn on a sixpence. Delta guys use them extensively in ops. When we were going in to extract the British Ambassador from Zaire, all the embassies were being closed down because of widespread riots and killings. For our mission we had a single Gemini inflatable boat with a leak in it to cross the River Congo. But the Americans had a Black Hawk and two Little Birds on stand-by for their extraction of the American ambassador. The Little Bird was extremely small and incredibly manoeuvrable, like a sports car, and was able to land in the garden of the US Embassy!

a fast-rope rappelling system, and can help to secure the LZ from the air with its dual 7.62mm miniguns, capable of spitting out up to 6,000 rounds per minute – enough firepower to put off even the most determined enemy combatant.

HH-60 PAVE HAWK // Designed for combat search-and-rescue operations behind enemy lines, and commonly used by US SF to rescue downed pilots, the Pave Hawk comes with a smaller payload and transports soldiers across short distances. It's capable of a maximum speed of 195 knots (224mph) and has an impressive cruise speed of 159 knots (184mph). Fitted with hi-tech radar warning receivers to alert it to possible detection, the Pave Hawk's stealth capability is backed up by flare/chaff countermeasures, night-vision goggles lighting and can be refuelled mid-flight thanks to a retractable probe. It also has top-notch mounted machine guns on the side windows or cabin doors.

HELICOPTER EXTRACTION

Helicopters are also a great way of getting operators out of the battleground, and fast. Their main advantage is flexibility. They can perform both landing extractions, and airborne. Airborne helicopter

Helicopter air assaults can be deadly effective. In the Iraq War, Chinooks were vital to the successful insertion of UK Special Forces into enemy territory, helping to secure vital oil and infrastructure targets and delivering the soldiers in larger numbers, and more quickly, than land vehicles or airplanes could have done. For that reason, they're the modern operator's preferred way of entering the combat zone.

extractions are known in the trade as Special Procedures Insertion and Extraction (SPIE).

LANDING // When there's a reasonably wide open LZ, and if the load is not too heavy, the helicopter can land vertically. But the SF team still has to be careful in choosing the LZ: when a helicopter is burdened with a heavy load of troops and equipment, taking off vertically again may not be possible. Then it has to edge forward like a plane, gradually nosing upwards. But the amount of space required is still tiny compared to the needs of a giant airplane. A Chinook needs around 150 feet radius to land, up to 200 feet by night – that's a whopping 800 feet less than required by a plane.

SF teams can also choose helicopter LZs on surfaces that aren't flat. Hills, mountains and slopes can be adapted by cutting down the trees and digging up the soil. This creates a smoothed-out area that can absorb the helicopter's weight when it lands, although the team has to be alert to the danger of the rotary blades striking against tree canopies. Light helicopters can also land on swamp or marshlands with the aid of artificial LZs – platforms constructed from gravel and timber.

Landing is only possible when the SF team has had time to create a suitable clearing. Often, in the heat of battle, airborne extraction by helicopter is the only option.

SPIE // In the Vietnam War, US Special Forces were desperate for a quick way to pull their guys out of the frying pan, so they designed the STABO (Stabilised Tactical Airborne Body Operations) Rig. This was an X-shaped harness slapped across the soldier's back. The helicopter's extraction line was strapped onto the two shoulder-mounted rings and the helicopter could then pull away (the guys would have to interlock their arms and legs, with the end man stretching out his arms to avoid the team spinning in the slipstream).

In my book, the updated SPIE system is better, and I'll tell you why. SPIE is a version that the Navy SEALs cooked up based on a US Army original. Anything that SF teams use is usually an improvement on the original, and that's just as true here. SPIE's genius is that it uses one rope instead of two, with a series of rings spliced several feet apart. This simplified design means that, in mid-air, the operators aren't bumping into each other, and more importantly that their hands are free to hold their weapons. No better way of saying goodbye than slotting a few of the enemy.

Helicopters are great for inserting and extracting troops. In tight, claustrophobic battlegrounds, being able to withdraw troops quickly whilst suppressing enemy fire can make all the difference.

The one drawback to helicopters is that they alert the enemy because of the noise they generate. In addition, they are vulnerable to ground fire – it only takes one guerrilla with an RPG to toast a helicopter. In situations where the ground threat is significant, or the team requires a stealth insertion, going in by airplane – parachuting – is the ideal solution. Planes have some advantages – they can fly higher, evading surface-to-air missile launchers and RPG attacks, they can fly at the same altitude as commercial airliners which can disguise their insertion and they can hold more men and equipment too.

PARACHUTING

Parachuting into the combat environment is a hugely difficult and complex challenge. High altitude temperatures can be as low as -50°F, and you risk frostbite, drowsiness, blurred vision, dull and numb muscles and ultimately – and fatally – losing consciousness. The training required for combat parachuting in is both intensive and takes a great deal of time. But the advantages are also massive: quick, undetected and precise insertion deep into enemy territory, speedier than it would take to cross the same land mass on foot, and without the strain of carrying a heavy equipment load the whole distance. With the correct training and using military technology to evade or knock out enemy radar systems, air insertion is a powerful way for Special Forces operators to go to war.

Parachute insertions go through four stages, commonly called the **Mounting Phase**, **Air Movement Phase**, **Assault Phase** and **Subsequent Operations Phase**.

MOUNTING PHASE // This covers the timeline from the order being given to plan for a mission, until the moment the aircraft leaves the runway to begin operations. This phase focuses on joint tactical and support planning, carrying out last-minute checks on equipment and supplies, and briefing the guys and crew on the mission objectives. At the end of the mounting phase, all the troopers and equipment are marshalled to the holding area and loaded onto the aircraft.

AIR MOVEMENT PHASE // The period of time from the moment the plane takes off until the delivery of units to the parachute drop zone (DZ).

ASSAULT PHASE // From the moment the operators jump from the aircraft through to securing the DZ and seizing any initial objective (e.g. a nearby radar station or outpost). The SF team is either dropped together from several different aircraft into the same DZ, or into different DZs, or the same DZ at different hours, depending on the conditions and enemy defence systems. The designated SF Pathfinders may be inserted ahead of the other jumpers, either using the same HALO/HAHO (see pp. 108-116) method, or sometimes an alternative mode of entry, either on foot, or via submarine to the nearest shoreline. This is so that the enemy isn't alerted to the delivery method of the rest of the special ops team, endangering the safety of the other lads.

In the British Army, Pathfinder Platoon (attached to 16 Air Assault Brigade) are charged with reconnoitring and marking and survey of the DZ or helicopter landing zone (LZ).

Once the Pathfinders have landed and established an airhead, they will perform a critical role in establishing communications with the aircraft, letting the pilots know of any unexpected ground obstacles to watch out for (such as identifying enemy ground-to-air mortar units which might not have been picked up on the original planning phase), and also updating the main team on any important ground data that will

During Operation Palliser in Sierra Leone in 2000, Pathfinders played a crucial role in the success of Britain's elite forces against the notorious militia the West Side Boys, a cowardly bunch who chopped the limbs off children. As well as gathering intelligence on the ground, Pathfinders were also used to create diversionary tactics: by carrying out patrols in some areas but avoiding others, they created a 'trap zone' that the West Side Boys fell for hook, line and sinker. Once they were trapped, it was game over.

help them during the jump (weather conditions, state of the DZ or LZ and information directly related to the jump such as wind velocity and direction). They'll be comfortable with using the latest technology (homing beacons, electronic navigational aids) as well as tried-and-tested old-school tricks (signal mirrors, smoke, flashlights) to direct aircraft towards the DZ or LZ.

SUBSEQUENT OPERATIONS PHASE // This is when the ground team continues the rest of the mission on foot, carrying out primary and secondary mission objectives before heading for the RV point for extraction.

FREEFALL

SF teams will use one of two types of military freefall to parachute into enemy territory: High-Altitude High-Opening (HAHO) and High-Altitude Low-Opening (HALO). Of the two, HALO is by far the more common method in use today, and one that I personally practised during my time in the Regiment.

HALO // is practised by elite units teams the world over. Invented by US Special Forces geeks in the 1950s, the HALO method enables operators to be covertly inserted into hostile territory, often under the

Every Special Forces outfit worthy of the name is able to perform a HALO or HAHO insertion. From the Australian SAS through to Singapore's SOF Commandos and the US Navy SEALs, it's essential. Most SF operations will involve HALO or HAHO insertion. It's the ultImate way of dropping in soldiers, equipment and supplies.

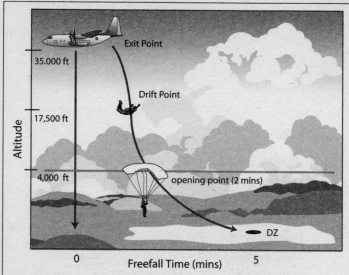

HALO is one of the fastest ways of insertion. Operators can cover literally miles in a matter of minutes, but the technique requires training to perfect.

cover of darkness. It's so effective because at 25,000-35,000 feet, the aircraft is flying at the same altitude as a commercial aircraft would be – and that could fool radar systems into thinking it's just another passing Boeing 747.

But the downside is that HALO requires a lot of planning and care during execution. Jumping from an incredibly high altitude can be lethal. When the human body is at that kind of height, oxygen is in short supply and can lead to hypoxia – a serious

In Afghanistan, where elite operators must insert into territory far beyond command centres to neutralise al-Qaeda and Taleban suspects, HALO has proved to be an effective and fast method of tackling threats.

Although it's pretty daunting at first, HALO is actually a very safe way of inserting SF teams into the operating environment. Having said that, there are times when it can go wrong. I knew this guy whose main chute didn't deploy on his first two jumps. Thinking the operator was doing something wrong, the instructor gave him an earful and joined him on the third jump. The operator's parachute opened fine this time – but the instructor's main chute and emergency chute both failed, and he plummeted to his death. The odds on that happening are shorter than winning the lottery ten times in a row, but that didn't stop the operator freaking out over the accident and transferring out of Air Troop.

condition resulting from a lack of oxygen in the bloodstream. Hypoxia can cause loss of consciousness, and if that happens during a HALO jump, the operator is in deep trouble.

In the Regiment, we trained for HALO jumps by spending two days at RAF Brize Norton, going through all the drills with the RAF boys. Safety drills are practised over and over and the operators also work on their balance technique – if your body isn't perfectly balanced you will start to turn or drift off course. The first jump will be from a C-130 Hercules, just the operator and the HALO instructor. He will jump out after the operator, making sure the student's body isn't unbalanced or over-arched during the freefall phase, as this causes the operator to fall faster.

It goes without saying that tabs, booze and drugs are off-limits: use of any of those substances in the previous 24 hours can make the soldier more susceptible to hypoxia. They will also spend half an hour or more prior to the jump breathing in 100% oxygen. This flushes any nitrogen out of their bloodstream. When the aircraft is in position, the team will free-fall together at terminal velocity. The maximum height they can HALO from is 25,000-

35,000ft typically. Using the starfish position the jumpers will steer themselves towards the team leader, until they reach low altitude and they deploy their chute at around 4,000ft and under canopy by about 3,000ft. With the chute open the jumper will direct his canopy towards the designated DZ. Equipment they bring along for the ride includes an altimeter (used to measure their altitude), an **Automatic Activation Device**, **AAD** (a safety device that automatically opens the parachute at the critical point of 2,000ft – any lower and it's too late), **gloves** and **free-fall boots** to protect against frostbite, and of course **Bergen** and **combat** gear which adds 100lb or so to the jumper's weight.

HALO allows SF teams to land together in groups, rather than being sporadically dropped across a wide area. HALO jumps are best conducted at night, under cover of darkness, giving the team the best possible chance of evading enemy forces. Having said that, HALO also allows teams to be dropped in multiple locations – meaning three teams can launch three separate attacks on the enemy at the same time, creating havoc in the enemy ranks.

HAHO // The downside to HALO missions it that the aircraft is required to fly into enemy airspace. With

HAHO jumps, because the team releases parachutes after only a few seconds in free-fall, the drop can be made over friendly territory, with the freefallers then using gliding and drifting techniques to slowly navigate towards the DZ. Wearing oxygen masks, the team makes the jump at 30,000ft and freefalls for several seconds. At 25,000ft, the parachute is deployed. GPS is used to help direct the soldiers towards the DZ. A HAHO jump can take more than an hour from exit to landing, and travel more than 30 miles towards their landing point. And because the jump is made much further away, the chances of alerting the enemy are much smaller. In the Gulf War, HAHO techniques were used a lot, so that the Iraqis wouldn't hear the airplanes approaching and let rip with some SAM (Surface-to-Air Missile) attacks.

HAHO parachutes are advanced bits of equipment. They use a self-inflating airfoil called a 'ram-air'. This is a parafoil (made of a complex cell structure called ripstop nylon which inflates into a wing-shaped cross-section) that allows the operator complete control of his descent in terms of speed and direction. If they used a normal parachute at 25,000ft, they would simply drift along aimlessly and hit the ground about ten minutes and three miles from the release point. The ram-air technique is much closer to paragliding and its aerodynamic properties allow the operator to stay in the air for significantly longer, up to an hour and therefore increasing the distance he can travel from the release point by up to 30 miles. In theory it's possible to release your chute in one country and land in another.

The biggest problem with HAHO is navigation, as the descent begins from much higher up, further away from the DZ, and it will probably be dark and possibly cloudy too (HAHO missions are commonly executed at night). GPS navigation systems are essential if the jumper is to avoid drifting off target and falling into enemy hands.

These are the two main parachute methods used by Special Forces for covert entry into enemy territory. Both methods help them avoid enemy radar defence systems and drop into hostile environments that would otherwise be very difficult to penetrate without setting alarm bells ringing.

HALO and HAHO inserts are usually carried out from the back of a C-130 Hercules aircraft. The C-130 is one of the most dependable aircrafts in the trade and it is used not just for airborne assaults, but also search and rescue, transport of troopers and supplies and as a resupply craft. It is capable of carrying more than 60 airborne operators, and has a maximum payload of 20,000kg, even allowing it to transport an M113 Armoured Personnel Carrier! As a gunship it's without equal and it's still in operation today, helping the lads in Iraq and Afghanistan.

Sometimes operators will need to help 'piggyback' someone into the combat zone (also known as tandem jumping). The jumper is attached to a person with little or no high-altitude parachuting experience using a specially rigged harness. I'd say this is pretty rare, and only used in cases where specialised personnel are essential to a mission's success, for example if the team needs to bring along a translator to communicate with locals, an informant to point out and identify enemy targets, or a nuclear scientist to identify nuclear weapons.

There is another way of dropping in, known as *static-line parachuting*, where a fixed cord is attached to the soldiers and the parachute automatically opens when they jump. Commonly used by the British Parachute Regiment as part of wider combat operations (e.g. a full land-scale invasion), the maximum jump height in training is 800ft, and on operations it's about 250ft. It's designed for operators to spend the least amount

Whether it's HALO, HAHO or static-line, the SF team is at the mercy of severe weather and challenging terrain. In Malaysia in the 1950s, the SAS lads even experimented with 'tree-jumping' – the idea being that you look for the tallest tree in the forest and let your parachute get stuck on it, and then cut yourself free to drop to the ground. It was a barmy plan, caused a lot of injuries, and didn't last long. But it just goes to show: Special Forces outfits will try *anything* to get into the best possible position with the least possible detection!

of time in the air so they're not a target. Static-line jumps from 250ft mean you're on the ground in seconds.

This isn't practical for dropping in without waking the neighbours; you can really only undertake static-line parachuting on a large-scale, when you've totally smashed the enemy's defences and have complete air superiority. It's also more likely to damage SF teams: according to one study, soldiers performing static-line parachuting in a combat situation were twice as likely to injure themselves. It was useful back in the Second World War. Less so now.

STANDARD OPERATING PROCEDURES FOR DZs

Dropping into enemy territory is seriously dangerous business. Any number of things can go wrong. And that can lead to capture, interrogation, or worse. In the Regiment we were trained to deal with the physical and psychological trauma of being taken hostage, and I can tell you from experience, it's not something any professional wants to suffer, no matter how hard and skilled he is. So it's vital the team is drilled to deal with the unexpected in any DZ:

MEET UP // Wherever the team drops, beforehand they will have all agreed on a meeting point. As a rule, this shouldn't be smack bang in the middle of the DZ. Behind some cover to the north or south of the DZ is ideal.

BE READY FOR ANYTHING // There's always the slight chance that the mission might be compromised before they've even touched down. The enemy might have got wind of their plans, or the aircraft might have been detected by defence systems. Sometimes it's even simpler than that. During the hostage crisis at the 1972 Olympics in Munich, border patrol cops dressed up as Olympic athletes and planned to launch an attack against the apartment housing the terrorists and the hostages. The attack was called off after the terrorists, watching TV, saw live footage of the cops approaching the apartment. So you never know how a mission might be compromised.

But you can prepare for compromise. When the team member hits the ground, they will have their weapons primed, anticipating contact. If contact does occur then the guys will set up a defensive baseline, concentrating fire to keep the enemy at the maximum distance. Depending on how strong the opposition force is, the team will have to decide whether to extract immediately, or take down the enemy and continue the mission. If it's a covert operation, there's a strong case for radioing in for an emergency extraction. How long that takes depends on the operation. When I was on patrol in Iraq, it was possible to fly in and pick us up over a period of two to three hours. In urban warfare environments, where the enemy is unseen and the team could be compromised in a matter of minutes, getting the guys out of a hostile civilian environment quickly is critical. Today in Baghdad, the lads have helicopters on standby that are only 5 or 10 minutes away. But if the operation is taking place in a more remote area, the time to run an emergency extraction increases. In Afghanistan the guys can call in and might have to wait several hours for a helicopter.

COVER YOUR TRACKS // Even if the team isn't greeted by a hail of bullets, failing to properly clear their tracks could spell danger down the line. If a patrol unit comes across a clearing littered with bits of parachute cord and footprints, it's going to be blindingly obvious that a covert team has penetrated their borders.

AIRBORNE RESUPPLY

Elite operators may be toughened by years of training and gruelling physical punishment, but that doesn't mean they're able to carry everything and the kitchen sink on their backs. When the team's on a long recce, there's little chance they'll be able to carry all the supplies necessary for remote operation. This means, at some point, they'll need resupply.

Resupply is usually conducted from the air by establishing a drop zone. SF teams need to take several factors into account when choosing a resupply drop zone. They need to consider drop altitudes and relay that information to the pilot, how built-up the area around the potential DZ is, how long the aircraft needs to spend over the DZ and how easy to access their chosen DZ is. It's no good choosing a big clearing free of obstacles if it's difficult to access and the surrounding area hasn't been properly recce'd.

Nowadays most airborne resupplies are carried out using the HALO technique.

HALO resupply involves the goods being dropped in from high altitude with each container's parachute opening at a low altitude for fast, effective delivery.

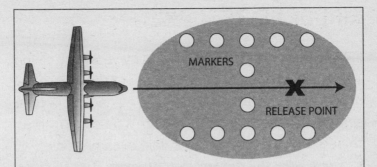

MARKERS

X

RELEASE POINT

When making a resupply the guys on the ground will drop a series of markers. The markers could be strobes, panel lights or flashlights and will be in the shape of a particular letter in a code word. If the wrong letter is displayed, the pilot will know that the mission has been compromised and pull out of the drop.

The SF team prepares a series of ground markers to indicate to the pilot where to drop the stuff. The markers can be flashlights, panel lights, strobe lights or 'beanbag' lights (ones that change colour). The team will also use the markers to construct a Ground Marking Release System (GMRS), which the team will use to identify to the pilot the release point. The pilot will then adjust his flight path accordingly.

US Special Forces use what's known as an Army Verbal Initiated Release System, where a code word is used over radio communications, with that code letter also being displayed at the release point. So, for

During the Second Gulf War, the success of US Special Forces was in part due to the effective aerial resupply of SF units operating in the field. A flexible delivery system, coupled with elite soldiers capable of locating an emergency drop zone or preparing a HALO drop site at short notice, meant that the soldiers were able to continue the fight.

example, if the code word is 'HEAT', the code letter might be 'H', constructed from light panels by day, or strobe lights by night.

The other common form of resupply is emergency drops. During the mission, the SF team will keep in regular radio contact with HQ. Once the team have missed a number of contacts (usually three or four, depending on how frequently they're checking in), then the head shed will decide that the team has been compromised and the mission aborted, that the lads are now in an Escape and Evasion (E&E) situation and drop emergency supplies into a pre-agreed drop zone. These emergency supplies will help the guys to stay alive and operational for longer – they will be moving with only their survival belts attached, having ditched their backpacks and weapons as part of the E&E SOPs. They'll be short on rations, short on equipment and short on guns – the emergency drop stuff will increase their chances of survival.

AIRCRAFT EXTRACTION

If everything's gone to plan and the mission objectives have been completed, the team can now prepare for extraction and the ride home. A recce team being pursued by enemy forces needs a quick

Getting out of the combat zone requires concentration, patience and planning. It's tempting to start thinking of getting back to a slap-up meal and a warm bed, but as an elite operator you have to push those thoughts to the back of your head.

way out of danger before they become pinned down in a firefight and will opt for helicopter extraction, but an assault unit that has successfully secured the area and eliminated its targets has the time and fighting advantage to set up temporary defences, make a brew and organise a smooth aircraft extraction.

Extraction points can leave the team vulnerable to attacks from sniper positions and entrapment. It's vital that the extraction point is scouted and cleared of enemy troops first. You don't want to be swapping rounds with the bad guys when your helicopter comes in to pick you up – the pilot won't hang around for long in such conditions, for starters.

Most extractions are nowadays performed by helicopter, as they're able to land in much more congested and difficult terrains at short notice. I've discussed helicopter extraction already above. But SF teams can, in some cases, extract by plane too.

For aircraft extractions, the team will need to build an airstrip. Their choice of extraction point is obviously limited to areas that are long and wide enough for aircraft landings (depending on the plane – a C-130 Hercules needs a shorter runway than other types of aircraft). Sometimes the land can provide natural

Urban environments present their own problems for extraction. When I was working alongside BOPE, I saw examples of how potentially dangerous extracting from an urban combat zone could be. Narrow streets and debris make it hard to find a decent extraction point, while shanty huts and high-rise buildings provide great cover to snipers.

The AK-47 is one weapon that every elite operator should know how to handle. Durable, cheap to manufacture, the Kalashnikov is used by armies, guerrilla forces and terrorists across the world, especially in poorer countries. Most operators will have to face one, as well as use one, during their Special Forces careers.

Magav operators have to be able to look, sound and dress like civilians in Palestinian territories. Protecting their identities is also vital otherwise their ability to operate clandestinely and effectively in a hostile terrain is compromised.

The 66 LAW. Great for bunker-busting or hitting lightly-armoured vehicles, or if someone's hidden behind a wall. Packs a punch.

The PP-19 'Bison 2', developed by the son of Mikhail Kalashnikov, is used by the Sunkar in Kazakhstan. The magazine is a worm-type fitted under the barrel and is designed to provide additional stability when firing.

The Pecheneg heavy machinegun is a support weapon ideal for use in Deliberate Action (DA) attacks such as airfield assaults. This is an Eastern European gun – the Regiment equivalent is the Browning .50.

The GM-94 can fire HE, smoke or thermobaric projectiles and is a devastating weapon. Projectiles are able to travel between 50-300m using a fixed sight to establish range. You can literally watch as the GM-94 lobs projectiles through the air. The kill range is 3m but I wouldn't stand twice that distance away. It's designed to kill everyone in a room through heat and overpressure. Thermobaric rounds have no fragmentation; they just suck your lungs out.

The RPG. Self-propelled, easy to fire, reload and cheap to produce and purchase, this is a very popular weapon amongst both operators and guerrillas and terrorists. Nowhere demonstrates that better than Iraq, where both Iraqi servicemen (left) and insurgents have used RPGs to devastating effect.

Whether it's with Mexico's Policia Federal, Israel's Magav or the Sunkar in Kazakhstan, having the right gear, guns and battle plan makes all the difference.

Helicopter insertion is a fast, effective way of getting troops onto the ground in environments that would otherwise prove difficult to access.

Australian SAS commandos
abseil down a series of
ropes. Their descent is much
more controlled than a fast-
rope insertion, and these
guys are carrying a serious
amount of gear.

space – a frozen lake or an open desert, for example. The job for the guys then is to clear away any debris and make sure the runway is smooth. An uneven, potholed surface can damage the plane's wheels and undercarriage and leave the unit, and the extraction team, stranded in the combat zone. The team will have to place strobe or panel markers around the site to direct the pilot towards the LZ. If the team has selected the wrong code letter (i.e. the panels are forming the shape of an 'E' rather than a 'T') then he'll abort the mission, so it's crucial that the team gets the signal correct.

Sometimes the only choice is to go in by foot or vehicle, even if you don't like it. When I was based with BOPE in Rio, the only way to enter the Wild West favelas, where the enemy was concealed and the randomly-built up structures made airborne insertion impossible, was using armoured cars known as Skulls. They were big and bulky, but vulnerable to petrol bombs. I hated being inside one – it made me feel like a sitting duck. There's no point complaining; you just accept it, and watch each other's backs at all times.

04 GOING IN BY OTHER MEANS

> SOMETIMES AIRBORNE INSERTION JUST ISN'T PRACTICAL. THAT'S WHEN THE HEAD SHED NEEDS TO START CONSIDERING ALTERNATIVE ENTRY METHODS TO THE COMBAT ZONE //

LAND

In the days before fast-roping in on a Black Hawk or HALO-ing from a Hercules became part of daily life for elite operators, going in over land was the most convenient and obvious way to enter into any hostile environment.

Going in on foot made sense in the days when SF teams mostly had to cross borders and contend with sophisticated enemy air and naval defences. That was the traditional role of land-based insertion. Nowadays SF teams use land insertion if the terrain they're entering is too isolated for helicopters or risky for

HALO insertion – if they don't know enough about enemy strength on the ground, getting soldiers to freefall in might land them in the middle of an enemy stronghold. In Afghanistan, soldiers learned to insert and get around on horses, because horses are low maintenance, can move over bumpy, dusty terrain, and are easier to 'refuel'. Chasing forces back across a border is another reason an SF team might choose land-based insertion. Again in Afghanistan, I've heard of US Special Forces teams launching cross-border strikes against high-value targets in Pakistan's South Waziristan region, which shares a border with Afghanistan and is a haven for the Taleban and al-Qaeda. The US SF lads would pursue the team to the border following an ambush then create a plan for a counter-insertion on the ground.

In the SAS we have Mobility Troop. They train extensively on every type of vehicle imaginable, from motorbikes to pinkies (Desert Patrol Vehicles). Mobility Troop lads are also trained in mechanics to an advanced level and can fix virtually any problem that arises on a vehicle – essential when the patrol is hundreds of miles from friendly forces. They also train in off-road motorbiking and rally driving, fast-driving (basically driving vehicles at breakneck speed), vehicle recovery drills, driving with Night-Vision Goggles and

The Supacat M-WMIK (M-type Weapons Mount Installation Kit) vehicle is used by British operators in Afghanistan and Iraq and is a superb weapons support platform, kitted out with enough firepower to suppress and neutralise enemy targets whilst retaining excellent mobility and reliability in extreme terrain. It comes fitted with an internal roll cage to protect the three-man crew, a crew protection mount (CPM) – a GPMG fitted to the front of the vehicle to allow the operator to provide an arc of fire and protect the crew when the vehicle is static, and a Folding Interface mount – a rear mounted .50 cal to put serious rounds down on targets. The .50 cal heavy machine gun is an exceptional piece of equipment, capable of laying down rounds at distances of up to 2,000m. The guys operating the vehicle will normally fire the weapons in sequence, with a 2-3 round burst from the .50 cal being followed up with a similar burst from the front-mounted Gimpy to create sustained, lethal fire on enemy positions. The M-WMIK can also be kitted out with twin Gimpys for an extremely high rate of fire and a Javelin ATGW (Anti-Tank Guided Weapon).

in different formations. They'll brush-up on their drive-by shooting skills, practising using heavy weapons and machine guns and grenade launchers, mounted on the vehicles, to take out moving targets, or lay down fire whilst they're on the move themselves.

In difficult terrain sometimes it's best to move in by vehicle. For example, inserting on foot into arctic environments can be exhausting and slow, whereas specially designed snowcats can move with relative ease, helping the team to reach an RV point from which they can carry out the mission objectives. In desert ops, pinkies are ideal for long-range patrols – the name 'pinkies' comes from the fact that Blades painted the Land Rovers pink, a colour which helped the vehicles blend into the scenery in the desert. Armoured Personnel Carriers (APCs) are developed specifically to transport operators to the frontline, as well as performing recces and security details. Vehicles can also serve a purpose in actual mission objectives, providing fire support and putting rounds down on enemy targets during a stronghold assault.

In environments where the roads are under-developed and tend to consist of winding rock-strewn lanes, getting around on a motorbike is better. This is how the Sri Lankan Special Task Force guys operate as

In Kazakhstan I got to ride in the BTR-80, a Soviet-manufactured armoured personnel carrier used by the Russians in Afghanistan and Chechnya and designed to cope with rugged, unpredictable terrain. Fast and reliable, the BTR-80 is capable of surviving a landmine attack, has two mounted 14.5mm cannons for putting rounds down on the enemy, and is fully amphibious. When I was in the Regiment we'd sit on the Kazakh border and spot these vehicles. But I never thought I'd get the chance to actually sit in the cockpit of one.

their combat environment consists of narrow, pot-holed jungle paths where larger vehicles would have difficulty navigating. Motorbikes have the advantage of quick manoeuvrability.

ANTI-PERSONNEL MINES

In countries that have been war zones for decades, anti-personnel mines are everywhere and present a real danger to teams inserting on the ground. This is particularly a problem when the insertion is taking place over a border between two countries who really hate each other. Afghanistan and Iraq are good examples of the terror of minefields. In Afghanistan there are a lot of mines in the ground dating back to the 1970s, relics of the Soviet-Afghan war. Iraq's border with Iran is littered with mines everywhere following the bloody Iran-Iraq War.

There are two main types of anti-personnel mine. Blast mines aren't designed to kill, because the medical and evacuation burden on the rest of the patrol of an injured soldier is thought to cause more logistical problems. They are pressure-activated, so when a patrol member steps on it, their foot or leg is blown clean off. Fragmentation mines use shrapnel to 'frag' a wider blast radius. In broad terms this means

Whatever the mission and whatever the terrain, you wouldn't want to make an approach over a minefield – it's too risky and even with painstakingly slow movement and the use of scanners, it's still possible to miss a mine and get blown to pieces. But at least intelligence can help SF teams avoid the areas littered with anti-personnel mines.

that if the point man in a four-team patrol activates it, the resulting frag is likely to maim or kill his comrades too. These can be activated by tripwires.

Detecting landmines during insertion is a painstaking process. Troopers will have to cover the ground by using scanners similar to the metal detectors civilians use for combing beaches. The alternative is to use satellite imagery and other intelligence to pinpoint possible landmine sites – if the ground has been disturbed recently it will show up on satellite, but this only works for more recent plantings of mines. If the SF team is inserting past local friendly villages, kids running around with missing arms or legs will alert them to the fact that there's probably a minefield somewhere nearby – and the locals can help them identify the area where people have been injured.

CROSSING THE FRONTLINE

In some situations, a Special Forces unit will be required to cross a war zone, penetrating into the territory of the opposing armed forces. In this case the problems SF soldiers face are very different: the 'border' or no-man's land is unlikely to have any advanced detection systems, simply because the enemy will not have had time to set up anything other than a rudimentary defence system. But they will be operating in an area of extreme hostility, amidst an area of concentrated enemy strength and firepower and one on the look-out for soldiers trying to breach their interior security.

Here the team's best chances of entering undetected is to dress up like the enemy. During the Soviet-Afghan war, Spetsnaz teams dressed as locals, pretending to be shepherds. More recently, SF operatives have been known to dress up as local men in Iraq, wearing Arab headdresses, carrying local weapons, and driving a car that a typical Iraqi civilian owns. That way they can continue their mission without arousing the suspicion of the enemy forces – or, in the case of Iraq, bloodthirsty guerrilla forces with no formal connection to the elected government. In other war situations, the operators may have to dress in the enemy's uniform, insignia, and even learn their language.

I've talked about **Land** and **Airborne** infiltration, as these are the most popular ways for going to war for hardened Special Forces teams. Going in on the ground can be tough, but effective. Air insertion is the

Sometimes going in on foot is best. In 1981 rebels in the Gambia launched a coup d'etat against the government of Sir Dawda Jawara. The capital, Banjul, was overrun and Jawara's family was held hostage. To help restore Jawara to power and protect the lives of British citizens caught up in the chaos, two SAS operatives were chosen to head to the Gambia and get the situation sorted.

The operators were flown into Senegal, which shares a border with the Gambia. Armed with grenades, Heckler & Koch MP5s and Browning Hi Power pistols, they walked over the border dressed in t-shirts and jeans. Once across the border   >>

they hooked up with a local ex-SAS Major based there. Making contact with Senegalese forces dispatched to end the rebellion, the operators formulated a plan to take back the city. Slowly the tide turned against the rebels. They led an assault against the radio station and the police armoury, running through the city streets, rounding up rebels and handing them over to the Senegalese forces. They also went to the local hospital – where they learned Jawara's family was being held – dressed as doctors and disarming the rebels. With the situation on the ground calmed down, the rebels crushed and Jawara returning to the Gambia, the SAS operators called it a day and flew home.

most covert way of entry into hostile territory. There's one other way of getting into a combat zone, used by another specialist part of the SAS, the Boat Troop.

SEA

Waterborne infiltration is a specialist skill. Negotiating natural coastlines and beaches, and carrying out attacks on harbours and port installations, requires constant training, and a lot of Special Forces have expert teams that are created specifically with water-based operations in mind. In US SF, there are six Operational Detachments A, or A-teams, in each SF company, and one of the six will be trained in Combat Diving. Other American forces also have specially trained frogmen and divers, including: Navy SEALs, Delta Force, and the Marine Corps' Special Maritime Purpose Force.

In the Regiment Boat Troop performs the function of Naval Special Warfare, along with the SAS's sister service, the Special Boat Service (SBS). Formed during the Second World War, the SBS are based down in Poole, Dorset, and their motto is 'By Strength and Guile' (catchy, but not as good as 'Who Dares Wins'). There's an intense, competitive rivalry between Boat Troop and the SBS, but it only helps to make both outfits sharper, fitter and better placed to tackle maritime threats. The two teams do a lot of cross-training too, and I'm proud to say that the guys in Boat Troop have the same skill sets, to the same level, as SBS combat swimmers. Both SBS and Boat Troop operators are known as 'swimmer canoeists'. They specialise in infiltrating behind enemy lines by boat, submarine, Klepper canoe (a non-metallic canoe designed for a two-man crew), helicopter or by HALO/HAHO parachute drop. Their expertise with waterborne insertion means they are ideally suited to launching assaults against coastal installations such as enemy ports and radar stations. Other roles they perform include:

★ Coastal and beach reconnaissance
★ Insertion and extraction of patrols by boat
★ Recovery or protection of ships and oil installations
★ Waterborne Counter-Terrorism
★ Underwater demolitions

In addition to regular Special Forces skills training, Boat Troop recruits need to demonstrate their ability in specialist exercises. They have to swim underwater for miles in low visibility, practise helicopter landings on ships in stormy conditions and endure survival training in the Scottish wild including carrying Klepper canoes across several hills before paddling in them for thirty miles, by themselves, along a Scottish loch. Boat Troop guys need to have lats and shoulders like body-builders to cope with all the long-distance rowing.

Specialist training also means specialist equipment. A combat swimmer will have a variety of hi-tech boats and diving gear they use on particular missions.

WET AND DRY SUITS // Wet suits are made
from neoprene and preserve body heat by trapping a layer of water against the skin. The water is warmed by body heat and insulates against the cold. Dry suits work on the opposite principle and prevent water entering, providing better insulation, and are therefore employed in deeper water dives when temperatures fall below 15 °C. Both are produced in a dark colour to aid stealth movement and are tough enough to resist scrapes and impact without tearing.

COMPASS BOARDS // Polymer boards fitted with
a depth gauge, compass and watch, are universally used by combat swimmers. Some more advanced models also have GPS fitted.

KLEPPER CANOES // Okay, so this is only hi-tech
if you're in the Stone Age, but despite being a bit old-

fashioned, canoes are still an effective and covert way of getting small units into enemy coastlines and riverines. Klepper canoes can be broken down into two parts so that the two-man crew are able to carry half of the canoe each on their backs when they go tabbing on terra firma. Kleppers are pretty flexible too, with the ability to be launched from boats, submarines (when on the sea surface) and from the air by parachutes or out of helicopters like the RAF Chinook. Sometimes the simplest solution is the best.

INFLATABLE RAIDING CRAFTS // Powered by diesel motors, these rubber craft are mobile enough to be dropped into position by aircraft, or launched from submarines. The craft can inflate rapidly thanks to compressed air cylinders. The big advantage with these craft is that combat swimmers can use the motor for travelling long distances when stealth isn't an issue, conserving energy, and then switch to paddles when approaching a coastline or waterway, enabling a more covert approach.

RIGID INFLATABLE BOATS (RIBs) // The hulls on these boats are made from glass-reinforced plastic (GRP), making them incredibly light but also very durable and capable of achieving a maximum speed of 35 knots and a max range of 200 miles. They can be launched a good distance away from the beach and without alerting land-based enemy forces. 12.7mm machine guns and Mark 19 grenade launchers can be mounted on the RIB to provide covering fire during an insertion or putting rounds down on a surprise river ambush during a patrol. Highly dependable, RIBs can carry more than a dozen combat swimmers.

RIGID RAIDER CRAFTS (RRC) // Like the RIB,

has a hull built from GRP. Can be air-dropped into the sea from the back of a Chinook or via a maritime freefall. Light enough that a team can carry the RRC when it reaches dry land, it's still capable of doing around 35 knots on its diesel engine.

MINI-SUBS AND SWIMMER DELIVERY VEHICLES (SDVs) // Powered by electric motors

running on zinc batteries, these are launched underwater and can hold between four and six men. Ideally suited to launching from submarines at a distance from the target site, or Beach Landing Site (BLS) – some SDVs can travel up to 36 nautical miles with a six-man crew. Mini-subs are often used for transporting sabotage teams to the shore. As they are underwater, they're a more clandestine alternative to waterborne boats and craft, especially when approaching a maritime counter-terrorism target, such as a pirate ship. The Navy SEALs use a similar vehicle, the MK VIII SDV. On-board navigation systems allow the team to navigate accurately to their target destination. These also come with fitted breathing systems, meaning the divers don't have to eat into their personal oxygen supplies during the approach phase.

AIR-CUSHIONED LANDING CRAFTS // Known on Civvy Street as hovercrafts, these lack the stealth functions of inflatable boats, but they are good for the rapid insertion of a large number of operators into a combat zone, if size and speed of the insertion force is the priority and the mission is not covert-dependable.

LADDERS AND HOOKS // There are two types of ladder that are designed for maritime combat. Collapsible ladders are used when combat swimmers are trying to board docked vessels. Caving ladders are used for the same purpose but are specially designed for launching an assault that requires speed. The grappling hook is the Hollywood option. This hook is attached to the end of the climbing rope. A rocket launcher or a compressed air rifle fires the hook forward, over the ship's railings.

REBREATHERS // Combat divers need to be able to stay underwater for extended periods of time, and without alerting the enemy to their presence. Standard commercial scuba gear is not suited to a combat environment, because it uses an open-circuit system that blows out bubbles, as well as emitting a 'hissing' noise when the diver is breathing in and out. The bubbles could be spotted by shore patrols as well as scout diving teams, and the same is true for the noise. For covert missions they will use Closed-Circuit Rebreathers (CCRs). These recirculate exhaled breath by cleaning it. By doing this no air is expelled into the water and no bubbles are created. The hissing noise of commercial rebreathers is also cancelled out. The most common rebreather system for combat swimmers is the LAR V Draeger. Its covert nature means that it's best suited to shallow waters close to the enemy coastline, where the chances of enemy patrols, and therefore detection, are much greater. The gas blend is usually pure oxygen. If you're running on pure oxygen you don't need to worry about decompression or nitrogen fatigue.

SUBMERSIBLE RADIOS // Technology is so advanced these days that units are now available, used by the SEALs and other maritime operators, which allow the team to maintain radio contact with each other and with HQ, even when underwater. The SEALs' Miniature Secure Hand-Held Radio (MSHR) is effective to a depth of 66 feet and allows both standard and encrypted communication. Comms gear is usually incorporated into the diver's full face mask.

Spetsnaz have their own equivalent of the SBS, called the SpN PDSS (which translates as Anti-Diversionary Forces and Means). The Russians are a secretive bunch, and little is known about this except that each unit has around fifty combat swimmers, and they are specially trained in anti-sabotage techniques (i.e. eliminating foreign frogmen trying to launch attacks against Russian naval bases). During the 2008 invasion of Georgia, SpN PDSS swimmers attached to the Black Sea Fleet carried out attacks against torpedo and missile boats inside Poti harbour in Georgia.

SpN PDSS equipment:

'PIRANHA' MINI-SUB // A two-man SDV designed for use in missions against moored ships, harbours and coastal installations. It has a maximum range of 50 nautical miles and can travel at a speed in excess of 7.5 knots. The Piranha has an on-board navigation system that uses GPS and Acoustic Doppler Velocity Log (DVL) – sonar that records water currents.

'SIREN' MANNED TORPEDO // Built by the Soviets after the end of the Second World War, this is a two-man torpedo that is launched via a submarine's torpedo tube.

APS UNDERWATER ASSAULT RIFLE // In maritime warfare, ordinary guns are about as much use as water pistols. Bullets are affected by the currents and become inaccurate and short-range. The APS, modelled on the AK47, uses a steel bolt 5.66mm calibre bullet from a non-rifled barrel that uses hi-tech hydrodynamics to keep the bullet in a straight line. Because of the specialised barrel though, the APS is redundant on land, so the Spetsnaz diver has to carry two guns, one for sea and one for land. It's also bulky and a bit fiddly, but in an underwater gunfight, the rifle is dependable enough to bust through an enemy diver's rebreather or helmet and send them packing.

SPP-1 UNDERWATER PISTOL // In close-combat underwater, SpN PDSS boys prefer the SPP-1 pistol. This uses cartridges rather than specially-adapted bullets – 4.5mm steel darts – and has a smart design, coming with four barrels that fire a cartridge each (a magazine holds four darts). The only downside is that it's not so effective at depth, because the higher pressure increases the

hydrodynamic drag on the round, so it's best used in relatively shallow waters.

IDA71 REBREATHER // Russian-designed, this is constructed with the emphasis on keeping the rebreather as streamlined as possible. If you take a scuba kit that tourists use on holidays, a quick look at the design shows how unsuitable it is to combat operations. The valves are located on the back of the tank, meaning that an attacker, above the diver, could turn the oxygen supply off and the diver would have a real tough time trying to reach round and turn it on again. And the breathing tubes, or aqualungs, are also highly exposed. A combat knife could slash through the tubes like butter. The IDA71 has a smooth backpack with no protruding features, the on/off switch is located near the bottom to protect the diver and the breathing tubes can be tied to the shoulder straps, keeping them packed in tight.

The US SF equivalent of Boat Troop and the SBS is the Navy SEALs. They're probably the most famous Naval Special Warfare outfit in the world – which isn't surprising, since American operators are as loud and yee-hah as they come. But the rigorous training and special equipment needs of the SEALs gives a good idea of the qualities needed to be an expert in waterborne combat operations. Prospective SEAL candidates first have to undertake a programme called the Basic Underwater Demolition/SEAL (BUD/S) screening test – a sort of naval version of Selection, intended to separate the ones who've got it from the ones who don't.

The BUD/S begins with a five-week course of 'Indoctrination and Pre-Training', comprised of a series of beat-the-clock tests, including a 500-yard swim with breast stroke or side stroke in less than twelve-and-a-half minutes, fifty sit-ups in under two minutes, and a one and a half mile run, in full combat gear, in less than eleven and a half minutes. Candidates then move on to the three Phases of BUD/S. Phase I is arguably the toughest, a physically and mentally gruelling series of conditioning exercises including the notorious 'Hell Week', five and a half days of brutal training that exposes students to life as a SEAL: swimming, paddling, surf passages, all whilst enduring being soaked in cold water, deprived of sleep and battered by freezing ocean winds.

Phase II focuses on diving skills and swimming techniques, dealing with issues such as dive physics and Phase III is all about land combat skills, involving weapons training, demolitions and other SOPs for

One of the most terrifying experiences I've had was during a waterborne insertion. I was out in Southampton training with a mate, when a ferry came passing over. It was dicey – we were trying to navigate from one side to the other, absolutely covered in silt and unable to see a bloody thing. We couldn't even tell which way was up or down. When you're blind like that, you have to trust the compass board.

Torpedo insertion is not for the faint-hearted, or the claustrophobic. Rising to periscope depth, you're placed inside the torpedo tube and then the hatch is battened shut. Then comes the hair-raising part – the tube is flooded and you swim out. This is great for stealth – but not so good if your idea of hell is being stuck in an elevator.

land warfare. Unlike the SBS, who recruit a lot of guys from land-based units, most SEALs lack an infantry background. They'll learn the more advanced land-based warfare techniques during an eighteen-week programme called SQT (SEAL Qualification Training) where they will study hydrographic reconnaissance, communications, combat swimmer skills, maritime operations and navigation, and inserting and extracting to submarines.

Submarine insertion can be performed using the float-on and float-off (flo-flo) technique. In flo-flos, the sub rises to periscope depth and the boat 'floats' onto the top of the sub. The combat swimmers then strap the boat down to the sub and enter through the hatch. At a later point the sub can then drop the guys off again, rising to periscope depth, discharging the Boat Troop guys, who then unstrap the boat.

Combat swimmers can also be deployed using wet jumps, where the team is inserted either using HALO freefall or deployed out the back of a Chinook onto the high seas. The boat is loaded onto a pallet, and it gets pushed out before the jumpers. When the guys hit the water they need to locate the pallet and cut the cords off their own chutes before untying the boat. This can be a pretty dangerous method of

One of the most important features of Special Forces is their adaptability to fighting – and surviving – in wildly different terrains and climates. In the Regiment we were taught how to fight in jungles so hot you could hardly breathe – but it was cold-weather training that helped me survive subzero temperatures for days on end during my escape from Iraq. Boat Troop and the SBS as well as Navy SEALs units might be specially trained for water ops, but that doesn't mean they can slack off from being prepared for land-based combat.

insertion – if you don't cut the cords properly, they can wrap around your legs and drag you down. That's what nearly happened to one guy in Boat Troop on a training exercise I was on; if his mate hadn't spotted the cord wrapped around the guy's ankle, he would have been wet toast. Navy SEALs employ a version of the wet jump known as the 'rubber duck' – the 'duck' being a Zodiac boat (a small inflatable boat that can be fitted with a motor) pushed out of the back of a C-130, followed by six SEALs who freefall down with it. The advantage here is that the team can carry the Zodiac when they move ashore.

It's vital that Naval Warfare operators are able to carry out a variety of different missions, because waterborne operations, the targets, and equipment needs of the SF unit vary wildly, depending on the mission objective. But generally speaking, most waterborne missions fall into one of four categories: **Recce**, **Rescue**, **Raid** and **Counter-Terrorism**.

RECCE

Coastal – or beach – recce involves swimmer canoeists and specialist boat teams carrying out surveillance work on the enemy beach and coastline before launching an assault or covert mission. These can be fairly straightforward or extremely complex, depending on the area identified for survey and possible attack. If the enemy has got its defences in order, it'll have also put mines and other obstacles along the coast and beach, and the recon team's job will also be to clear these mines and pave the way for the main patrol's insertion, making it as smooth as possible, and ensuring they've got as much detailed information as possible. Take it from me, when you're going on a dangerous mission behind enemy lines, the last thing you want is a nasty surprise on insertion.

To carry out a beach recce, the team will need to perform what's known as a hydrographic survey, and this begins with combat swimmers splitting up into pairs, with a guide pair in the middle of the group. The combat swimmers will be inserted offshore by fast boats using a cast and recovery procedure. The fast boat, or patrol boat, has an IBS (Inflatable Boat Small) attached to it. The combat swimmers roll onto the IBS and then into the sea. Generally they will perform the insertion at night time when visibility is low.

Once the guide pairs are in position, they give the signal and the combat swimmer pairs swim at a slow speed back and forth towards the beach in a loop. As they swim, the pairs will use a lead line to measure the water depth (a lead line is a lead sinker attached to a rope marked in one-foot increments). They will also dive to the bottom of the seabed to collect samples, keeping noise level to a minimum by adopting the jackknife dive, pushing themselves underwater using their upper body. This way they don't create a ruckus by splashing with their fins against the surface of the water. The beach recce team will also take notes about any obstacles, either natural (such as mud, jagged rocks or coral reefs) or man-made (including underwater mines) and also compile a detailed report of shore currents, which they do by placing an object in the water and watching it drift with the current. After sixty seconds or so, the combat swimmer will be able to calculate the current speed (all nautical speeds are measured in knots, 1 knot is equal to 1 nautical mile, or 1.852 km per hour).

Some combat swimmers now carry a system called DEBRA (Diver's Electronic Beach Reconnaissance Aid). This is a rugged, portable, two-handed console which floats on the water and comes equipped with GPS, an electronic compass and a depth sensor. Previously GPS antennae would stand out like a sore thumb but on the DEBRA system the antenna is camouflaged and attached to a buoy to prevent it rising to the surface and possibly being detected. DEBRA can function up to a maximum depth of 30m and can detect objects up to 20m below the surface. This system allows combat swimmers to build up an even more comprehensive picture of the offshore area.

Once the water stage of the hydrographic survey is completed, the team will move onto the beach for additional recon.

The combat swimmers will also keep a close tab on the surf by monitoring the pattern of waves breaking against the beach, working out whether the surf is dangerous or gentle.

When carrying out a beach recce, each member of the patrol will have a clearly defined role:

Officer in Charge (OIC) directs the beach recce operation. He's the guy responsible for organising when the patrol assembles for offshore pickup.

Boat keeper(s) keep a sharp look-out for any sign of enemy detection. Usually one or two guys, depending on the size of the patrol, they guard the IBS as it's the team's only ticket out to sea and safety.

Recce work might sound boring compared to action-packed assault operations behind enemy lines – but it's critical to any mission's chance of success. After all, there's only so much to be learnt from airplanes flying overhead. You need eyes and ears on the ground too, and the data they provide can mean the difference between success and failure – or life and death.

Cartographers will check out what lies on the beach, and beyond. They'll take photographs, obtain samples, make maps and sketches of anything of note, whether it's a possible enemy location or a potential LZ or DZ for an airborne insertion team. The information they collect has a massive bearing on the mission planning phase.

Swimmers can't bask in the glory just yet – they still have a task to do after the hydrographic recce job. Lying around the high-water mark area of the beach (the point where the high tide reaches furthest into the shoreline), they will measure the beach gradient and note other shore details.

Recce work done, the OIC orders the team to reform in a line and the team extracts using the same cast and recovery procedure only in reverse (transfer from sea to IBS to patrol boat).

RESCUE

These form part of the wider Combat Search and Rescue (CSAR) role of Special Forces teams. If airborne combat or surveillance ops are happening near to the coast, then there's a chance that the airmen could end up stranded from friendly forces. It's then a race against the clock for the Naval Special Warfare team to reach the downed pilot in time. The pilot won't necessarily have been downed over a body of water though; if the airman is downed on an island, or somewhere accessible by coast or river, then the NSW team will still be called on to carry out the mission.

Rather than wade in with a helicopter and full SF patrol and risk further casualties (remember, the pilots are probably downed deep behind enemy lines, and may even have fallen into enemy hands), the team will send an advance unit of one or two scout swimmers. These guys will find the downed pilot and then, using radio comms, coordinate aircraft or ground or boat forces on the rescue mission.

Maritime CSAR missions can play a major role in the rescue of troops. In the Gulf War, one US Air Force pilot had to bale out over the Gulf itself. A rescue party of two Navy SEALs launched from an SH-60B helicopter and discovered the downed airman a few miles out from the Kuwaiti coast. Jumping into the water to the pilot's aid, the SEALs attached a rescue harness to him and the SH-60B successfully winched all three men to safety. From start to finish, the entire CSAR mission had taken just over half an hour – far quicker than any land-based rescue.

RAID

Raids can take the form of 'shallow' attacks against the coastal area, such as sabotage of naval installations or military ports, or 'deep' raids, i.e. covert insertion down a river system for an assault deep into enemy territory. These are an excellent way of carrying out attacks that catch the enemy off guard, but river raids are complicated to pull off.

The first part of any raid is the covert insertion of the team, where submarines normally assist the team into enemy territory. The only exceptions are situations where a wet jump is necessary, or when the SF team can swim underwater to the shore. I've already described the hazards facing wet jumps, and the problem with swimming underwater to the shore is obvious: it's going to leave the swimmers shattered, and they'll only be able to swim a short distance compared to the nautical miles that boats can cover in the same time. Submarines are the combat swimmer's best friend. They can deploy combat swimmers on the sea surface or river bed, in either SDVs or manned torpedoes, by using dry-deck shelters specially fitted onto the submarine's hull for underwater deployment or modified torpedo launchers for manned torpedoes. If the team is using boats or canoes, these are sometimes towed by a submarine travelling at periscope depth, or when the sub has to go deep to avoid detection, sent to the surface using an inflated buoy, along with the combat swimmers.

For coastal installation ops, the SF team will always try to use an underwater approach with an SDV, because boats, although convenient, have propellers that make a lot of noise, potentially alerting the enemy to the team's presence. They don't want to do that – at least not until they've blown up everything.

Sometimes the SDV or manned torpedo isn't practical for a shallow raid. If the team can't return to the parent submarine for one reason or another, they'll have to think of another way to insert. Leaving the SDV or other transport device behind isn't an option with the risk of it falling into enemy hands. There is one other stealth choice: the canoe. Entering in canoes like the Kleppers that Boat Troop use can be really effective. Any noise from the paddling efforts of the soldiers is absorbed by wrapping the paddles in plastic to dull the sound of them hitting the water. But the threat of capsizing is always there, and again, rowing is a physically intensive activity. Slogging your way along a river for long periods is tough even for super-fit Special Forces operators.

In either form of raid, the submarine takes the combat swimmers to about a mile or so off the shore. Again, this is best done under cover of darkness, to reduce the chances of the team being detected.

Coastal installation raids are launched by combat swimmers. Dropped off by SDV or boat or canoe a mile out from the target, the swimmers will stay in pairs, working on the old saying that two sets of eyes is better than one. As they approach the target, they will go underwater, making it extremely difficult for enemy forces to pick them up. At this point, the combat swimmer's mind is totally focused on creating as little disturbance as possible, and navigating to the target. He can minimise detection by using the currents to drift towards the target, getting around the need to kick his legs to swim and so making traces in the water.

Once the SF swimmers locate their target – let's say here that it's a medium-sized naval ship – they can destroy it in one of two ways. The first is to use a laser target designator. This works in the same way as ground-based airstrikes: the swimmer uses a laser to paint the target, and a smart bomb is then dropped from the air onto the target. This method depends on the armed forces having air superiority.

Or the team can resort to the good old-fashioned way of sneaking up, attaching some explosives and giving the enemy a little fireworks display. Lugging a heavy load of explosives around isn't ideal for combat swimmers – too much heavy gear and they'll be fighting a battle not only against the enemy but also against the sea, as the gear weighs them down, making it a real struggle to stay afloat or near the water surface. To lighten the combat swimmer's weight burden, they will be equipped with buoyancy bags. The bags are a really simple but effective design: filled with water, they become weightless when underwater, lightening the weight of explosives and other heavy equipment such as weapons and comms units.

At the planning stage, the team will have identified the weak point of the target. The type of ship and the size of it is important, but the real trick is find the location of the ship's key functions – the engine room, for example. A carefully placed explosive on the outer hull next to the engine room will put the ship out of commission, whereas blowing up the sleeping quarters might cause havoc, but won't eliminate the ship's ability to function. And that's the goal of the mission.

FIGHT TO WIN

River raids are an effective way of launching deep counter-insurgency attacks. Some rivers can run for thousands of miles into the interior of a combat zone, and are much harder for an enemy force to patrol and monitor. Rivers are also an opportunity to stop enemy resupply efforts taking place along the waterways, and also to prevent enemy shipments – in Latin America, waterways and rivers are used to transport drugs out to sea for sale in America. Stopping these drug shipments on the rivers is better than chasing them out in the vast expanse of open water seas.

For river raids, insertion is obviously limited to boats. There's just no other way of easily negotiating a river system. The choice the team can make is usually between propeller boats and inflatable boats. Sometimes Special Forces outfits use indigenous canoes or boats to cross local jungle waterways – using these boats means the team don't stand out like sore thumbs. Any of these types of boat can be paddled down the river, but the same problems remain: noise versus extremely slow movement. Although military boats have specially developed motors that reduce the noise as much as possible, it's still audible to the human ear, especially to a twitchy enemy scout on the lookout for foreign activity. Navy SEALs use a specially modified boat, the Special

Operations Craft-Riverine (SOCR), which is a high-speed boat designed for the insertion of troops over relatively short ranges. It's armoured, comes with machine guns and mini-guns attached and is ideal for negotiating tricky, winding waterways.

When it comes to mounting a river assault, the team has to contend with a lot of obstacles. The first is that waterways are generally highly exposed, leaving the boat patrol at the mercy of enemy scout teams and sniper platoons. If they're not careful, the guys could get picked off like sitting ducks. Natural obstacles such as 'dead water' (where freshwater lies on top of a separate layer of much denser saltwater, potentially grinding the boat to a virtual standstill) and overhanging vegetation and debris such as twigs and mud, can also disrupt the team's movement upstream. The nature of rivers means that avoiding total enemy contact is not always possible, and when that happens, the team has to be able to deal with the threat, survive intact, and continue the mission – a good reason why the SOCR is fitted with lots of guns!

Just as combat swimmers carry out recon and raids in pairs, so do river teams. One boat is designated as the 'lead boat' and will be ahead of the other boat. Moving at speed, the lead boat will come to a stop

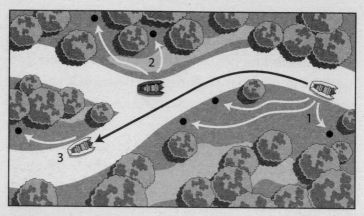

ALTERNATIVE AND SUCCESSIVE BOUNDS

Above: Alternative and successive bounds formations enable river patrols to move securely and avoid getting bogged down in an ambush, although it does mean the team sacrifices speed. In an alternative bounds formation the team has a designated lead boat whose operators debus at an observation point to recce the area ahead of them – 1. The guys in the rear boat now take over the role of lead boat and set up their own recce position further up, in an area that has been cleared by the guys – 2. The guys in the original scout boat now resume lead duties – 3.

when the crew reckon they're about to enter an area that could pose a threat. One of the operators will sound the alarm and the boat will come to a halt (the guys will be equally assigned to the left and right of the boat, charged with keeping a lookout for any possible threats). This system doesn't give the teams much of a chance if they are attacked, though, as both boats will still be in the water. Relying on the

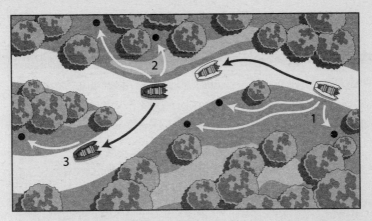

In successive bounds, the role of the lead boat is given to one boat rather than shared between the team, and their movement down the river is observed by the guys in the boat behind them – 1. This means the scout boat can debus at points 2 and 3, with the second boat always in a recce position to back them up.

---

crew's gut instinct about an area is also risky business, particularly if the river is winding, partially obscuring the view up ahead, or if there are islands hiding the waterway.

A more cautious method of river patrol is known as 'alternative bounds movement'. This is where one of the boats pulls up at the river bank and the crew disembarks onto terra firma. The team then take up a choice position to carry out surveillance of the area up ahead and provide fire cover for the second boat, which now moves ahead into the lead boat position.

FIGHT TO WIN

The new lead boat then lands at the bank side and sets up their own surveillance position, whilst the original recce team returns to their boat and again moves forward. It's slower than moving forward in standard lead boat formation, but it does provide better cover and the chance to spot enemy attacks.

There is an even more careful river patrol system called 'successive bounds movement', which is even slower than alternative bounds, but it's safer and better for really difficult waterways in very hostile enemy territory, where the team cannot afford, under any circumstances, to be detected or engage in any kind of combat. In successive bounds movement, a designated lead boat scouts out the area, landing at each potentially dangerous point and carrying out observation work. When the team is satisfied that the area is safe, they will signal to the second boat to move forward and join them. This second boat also disembarks, alongside the lead boat, and sets up surveillance position. The lead boat crew can now move forward, protected by the second boat crew.

For larger boat patrol groups, there are different formations available, just like for ground force patrols. As with the foot patrols, the formation used is at the discretion of the patrol leader. It's his responsibility to

Securing beaches is an instrumental part of modern Special Forces operations, especially when it comes to preparing for a large-scale ground invasion. In the Iraq War, SBS teams, working alongside US Navy SEALs, performed a critical role in securing the beaches along the marshy Al Faw peninsula that opens out onto the Persian Gulf, forming a beachhead to pave the way for the full-blown assault by coalition ground forces.

decide the best formation for the tactical situation facing his team. Once he has settled on the formation, he will communicate it to the rest of the team using hand and arm signals.

River raids are useful in a variety of mission scenarios – such as mounting ambushes against enemy positions or making a tactical withdrawal downriver once the assault has been successfully completed. This can be a standalone mission, or as part of a wider ground force attack on the enemy. In other cases, the insertion team will be required to provide detailed ground-level information on enemy combat strength, movement and weather to HQ in advance of an airborne or ground assault. They might also be required to secure a helicopter or plane LZ/DZ inland.

COUNTER-TERRORISM

Maritime counter-terrorism is an increasing problem, as terrorists and pirates conjure up ever more adventurous and depraved ways of inflicting damage on a country's infrastructure. Today's pirates are different to the old fashioned cartoon stereotypes. Now they're experts in hijacking oil liners, and using false papers to smuggle in boats rigged with explosives into densely populated harbours and ports.

Terrorists are also casting their nets wider and looking for new targets such as oil rigs and commercial passenger liners. In lawless countries like Somalia, pirating is a multi-million pound industry and civilian vessels are regularly captured by pirates off Somalian waters and its crews held to ransom.

Maritime counter-terrorism ops usually involve the SF team being deployed onto a moving object (such as a boat at sea), and are often carried out using helicopters. The helicopter will approach the target and hover over the boat. You need an incredibly skilled pilot with lots of hours of practise for this to work: with the ship bobbing up and down along the waves, the helicopter needs to constantly alter its height. The choppier the waves, the harder it is to carry out this landing. Once in position, the SF team will fast-rope down onto the vessel. Sometimes small boats will also be involved, approaching the target vessel from the rear and firing grappling hooks or caving ladders onto the ship and climbing up to the deck.

When onboard, the SF team will enter CQB mode, as a ship's corridors and compartments tend to be small, confined and dark. Targeting the ship's vital systems, they will split into teams and head for the bridge and

Assaulting moving waterborne targets isn't easy – but maritime terrorist threats are a genuine danger to national security, and teams like Boat Troop, the SBS and Navy SEALs are the guys who must stop them. In 2001, British intelligence was tipped off that a boat travelling towards the coast from Mauritius called the MV *Nisha*, was carrying suspected terrorist materials along with its sugar cargo. The Boat Troop and SBS lads sprang into action, deploying on RIBs whilst Lynx AH7 helicopters provided sniper support. Chinooks landed Boat Troop and SBS operators on the ship's deck, and the team quickly secured the bridge and radio rooms. Nothing dodgy was found on board the ship, but the MV *Nisha* incident is a great example of the bravery and rapid response of Boat Troop cooperating with the SBS to maritime terrorist threats.

engine room, as well as the area suspected by the team to be holding hostages. Entering each room they will use flash-bang grenades to disorientate the enemy, subdue terrorist suspects and gather together hostages. The team will make sure to use plastic handcuffs on the hostages as well; terrorists are a sneaky, cowardly bunch, and sometimes they'll pretend to be a hostage in order to facilitate an escape.

When it comes to inserting into enemy territory, whether by land, air or sea, Special Forces teams can overcome virtually any obstacle in their way. Using advanced techniques and equipment helps them insert covertly and quickly. And their natural cunning and resourcefulness as operators means that, when an SF team enters a hostile environment, you can rely on them to get the job done – and properly, to boot.

I can't emphasise how important it is for Special Forces operators to remain undetected in hostile environments. The mantra of Special Forces guys is that they fight at a time and place of their choosing – because they are relatively small teams, often heavily outnumbered and outgunned by the bad guys, it's vital that they hold the upper hand in detection and combat.

05 PATROL

> NOW THE TEAM HAS COMPLETED INSERTION, THE REAL ACTION CAN BEGIN //

Some missions will require the team to engage the enemy, call in air or artillery strikes, and even launch large-scale attacks by training indigenous forces into well-drilled and well-oiled army units – as British and American Special Forces did in Afghanistan, creating an irregular army to combat the evil Taleban and al-Qaeda network that had a stranglehold over the country's terrified population.

Other missions might sound less explosive, such as intelligence gathering or long range surveillance and reconnaissance, but these operations are just as important to the overall success of a military campaign.

SF teams will be trained to such a high level that they'll be expected to perform any type of operation in almost any part of the world to an incredibly high standard. In the SAS we specialised in long-range recce missions. They're extremely demanding ops as they require the guys to survive in extreme environments, undetected by large enemy forces, for long periods of time. And as well as staying hidden, we were expected to gather detailed information about the enemy force we were facing.

But we were also great at ambushes and raids, and search and combat rescue missions too. SF outfits have to be extremely versatile in order to cope with the many demands made of them by governments and regular armed forces desperate for their help.

Elite operator patrols can have four, five or more men. In the Regiment we used a four-man team that contained a navigator, linguist, medic and engineer (although, as I stated in the training section, every patrol member will be able to carry out at least two different roles in the team). Four-man patrols work because, when the team is in the shit, they can split into two-man firing teams and tactically pepper-pot back out of the ambush. The principle behind patrol contacts is 'shoot and scoot' – lay down fire and get the hell out of there before things turn ugly.

But to operate in any environment, they'll need to

know tricks and techniques to help them stay undetected, as well as some specialist tips unique to different types of extreme terrain.

Sorting out how the team is going to play it behind enemy lines depends to a large degree on the terrain. There are two sets of rules for negotiating enemy terrain – basic rules that apply to any combat zone, and special environment rules that apply to unique terrain conditions, such as the desert or jungle. I'll talk about the basic ones first, because these are the bread and butter of any SF operator's navigation skill set.

BASIC TERRAIN RULES

First and foremost, the SF team must remember that negotiating terrain is more than about arriving at the right place at the right time. It's about economy of movement and finding a route that provides the best observation points, the best cover, the best firing positions and doesn't expose the team to enemy attacks. In the real world, no such route exists and you have to find an acceptable compromise – one route might have the best vantage points but expose the team, another might offer more cover but make it difficult to carry out surveillance against the enemy.

Making the right decision about the best route can mean the difference between a successful mission and one that ends in disaster.

CONDITIONING

It goes without saying that all SF guys are rock-solid tough and made from granite, but they must be at the absolute top of their game for missions behind enemy lines. In addition to being able to tab long distances in relatively short timeframes whilst carrying heavy loads, operators must be able to climb mountains and negotiate difficult terrain whilst surviving on a negative calorie intake. If energy stores are low, the body starts to cannibalise muscle to burn, so the operator's muscle mass will deteriorate, and his sharpness and reactions will also decline. Over a period of several days of negative calorie intake his immune system will also weaken, exposing him to infection and viruses, depending on the environment the guy is operating in. To deal with these side-effects soldiers must not only be incredibly fit, at the same level as professional boxers or Olympic sprinters – they must also be mentally tough, able to push through the pain barrier, carry on with the task and get the job done.

CONCEALMENT

Camo is the obvious way of concealing Special Forces operators. Applied properly, camo can make soldiers virtually invisible in the field. I've already discussed the different types of camo available, and picking the right type of camo for the terrain the team is operating in is crucial. But there are other measures an SF unit can take to further decrease their visibility. Operators should follow the principles of **Why Things Are Seen – Shape**, **Shine**, **Silhouette**, **Shadow**, **Spacing**, **Movement**.

SHAPE // The shape of a human being can be recognised easily and almost instantaneously. The guys must make sure that their shape blends into the scenery. Helmets are particularly obtrusive against a skyline – camouflaging them with foliage and scrim netting is critical.

SHINE // Human skin, watches, wedding bands, normal rifle barrels all stand out against the dull colours of nature. Camo paint can cover up the skin and also helps to blur the outline of the soldier. Metallic objects such as watches and rings are banned; and guns are usually coated so they don't reflect the rays of the sun.

SILHOUETTE // Soldiers should be aware that smooth, undulating backgrounds mark out silhouettes easily to the human eye. If they are crossing in front of a river, a field or a skyline, the silhouette will stand out much more starkly than, say, against a dark woodland background.

SHADOW // SF patrols should understand where their shadow is being cast in relation to the direction of the sun and the movement of the patrol. Moving in areas already covered in shade (for example, directly under jungle or swamp canopies) is the best way to avoid creating obvious shadows. It's important to bear in mind that shadowed areas will change over the course of the day, in line with the movement of the sun.

SPACING // Objects in the natural world are spaced at irregular intervals. In a four-man patrol the distance between each operator should be different so they don't stand out as a pattern.

MOVEMENT // When hiding or performing a close-range recce, it's important for SF guys to have absolute muscle and breathing control. The human eye is prone to spot sudden or sharp movements, so if the operator does have to move, he must do so slowly, deliberately and cautiously so as not to arouse the suspicions of the enemy. Animals and birds can be antagonised or alarmed by sudden movements too, possibly alerting the nearby enemy to human contact.

In addition to these rules, operators will also usually carry their own waste with them. They'll do the business in plastic bags. They might choose to bury it, although if the topsoil is darker than the undergrowth, the difference in soil colour will instantly alert a tracker that a team was recently in the area. Carrying it in their Bergen is simple, but it's critical to keep excrement and urine in separate bags: mix them together and they can explode!

PACING

You'll occasionally hear stories of guys doing fifty or sixty miles a day in ten hours straight. Don't believe them. SF teams might travel that much distance, but if you did it without ample breaks, you'd soon be lying on the floor and unable to move, no matter how supremely fit you are. A quick rest, a brew and maybe a boil-in-the-bag meal or an energy bar, helps the team to recuperate and plan for the next leg of the journey. Breaking up the tab also provides the team with an opportunity to check its navigational

**In the Regiment it's all about
keeping it stupid-simple. Breaking
down pacing into 10m increments
keeps it as straightforward as
possible and reduces the chances
of something going wrong.
Stupid-simple is vital because the
lads are working under stressful
and arduous conditions, they're
knackered and they could become
forgetful. Overcomplicating things
could result in the mission being
compromised; keeping it stupid-
simple minimises the chances of
that happening.**

equipment and confirm that they're still on course to their rendezvous point or mission objective.

Pacing can be broken down to 10-metre increments. In SAS Selection training, students are often asked to glue a clicker-counter to the side of their rifle and click it every 10m, to teach them to map out their tabs in 10m increments. The reason pacing is broken down into 10m increments is that navigation in the jungle has to be precise and it's very easy to get lost and end up miles away from the RV. If you imagine a situation where a patrol member has to tab from a knoll to a ridge line and the distance is 100m. That's a lot of counting and the guy could get up to 78m, get distracted by a sound, and then think, 'Where the hell am I at?' If the trooper's pacing is 12 strides to get to 10m, on the 12th pace he will click and then count again to 12, then bang, click again. If he looks down at his clicker and it reads 7, he knows he's done 70m. Using GPS is usually not an option because of the thick overhead canopies that block satellite signals.

MOVING TACTICALLY ACROSS TERRAIN

Tabbing across mountains and hills and along streams is more energy-sapping than going across flat, open ground – but it's likely to be more concealed from enemy eyes. This has to be taken into consideration when deciding the best route to take. It's all about striking a balance. For hills and mountains, going straight over would create a silhouette against the moon during a night-time patrol, so it's best to negotiate the mountain at a point roughly two-thirds of the way up.

Teams shouldn't tab in a straight line. To throw off the scent of any enemy tracking patrols, they should double up and patrol in loops. They will perform a fish-hook manoeuvre, doing a loop to the left or right and doubling-up on themselves and hooking round to a previous point in their patrol route. They need to loop back a good distance so they don't bump into the enemy on their loop journey – the idea is that the guys can come up on the rear of any pursuing forces and launch a counter-ambush. For that reason the patrol will aim to double-up by at least 200m. When the team returns to its original track position they will look out for signs – a camp shit-pit, the smell of cigarette smoke or fresh footprints on the trail. Then they can begin to plan an attack against their trackers.

Loops should also be carried out prior to establishing a Lying-Up Point (LUP), to observe and anticipate any

'Sign' is elite operator code for anything that indicates the previous passing through of enemy forces. There are two types of sign that units have to watch out for. Top sign covers any markings or indicators that occur above knee-height such as the scars on trees made by careless rifle barrels or the bending of branches as backpacks have brushed against them. Ground signs are below-knee-height markers such as footprints, disrupted leaf patterns or discarded wrappings or cigarette butts. Electronic sign, classified as radio chatter between enemy team members or between the enemy unit and their HQ, can be picked up as well.

potential attacks on the team while they are at their most vulnerable, resting and having a scoff. Once they have surveyed the track and verified that it is clear of enemy forces, they will carefully move into the LUP, laying Claymores around the LUP perimeter as an extra line of defence against surprise ambushes.

Random changes in direction of the patrol also help to deceive enemy trackers – if the logical pathway from A to B is followed, it makes the trackers' job that much simpler. Going from A to B via C and D not only confuses the trackers, it also creates uncertainty about the team's RV.

Night patrols should be encouraged as this makes the team harder to detect. The downside, though, is that walking in the dark is going to be slower for the team. Open ground of any kind should be avoided at all costs. Roads, public paths, trading routes, mountain and hill tracks, are all highly exposed, likely to be bustling with civilians who may or may not be on the same side as the enemy forces, and could even be used by the military for supply trains and troop movement. Instead, operators should stick to covered areas (such as densely populated forests and hedgerows) to avoid detection. Operators must also take extreme caution to move as quietly as possible –

sound travels further at night due to the drop in humidity. Treading on a stray twig or stepping in a puddle is twice as likely to reach an enemy patrol's ears. Movement should be deliberate and controlled, feeling out the ground in front of the operator, and pausing frequently to observe the surrounding area. This is a very slow, time-consuming method of movement and requires great patience from the patrol members.

In some cases, motorways have to be followed. In a developing Middle Eastern country, for example, the motorway might be the only navigable feature in an otherwise flat, undulating desert environment, and the SF outfit will need to use it as a reference point. To navigate without attracting unwanted interest from the enemy, they'll work their way on a parallel path to the motorway, shadowing it but keeping a safe distance of around 150 metres between themselves and the road. Generally human eyes won't be able to detect them at this distance and they can safely follow the road towards the RV.

Whilst tabbing the SF soldiers must remain alert and keep their eyes, ears and noses sharp. In addition to looking-out for any possible enemy observation post positions, the team will need to listen out for any

Extreme caution has to be practised in the field: a careless sound, an erratic movement or the failure to erase all smells and signs of human activity from a rest stop, could endanger the Special Forces patrol. It just goes to show: the guys must be more than super-fit and good with guns. It's what they do when they're not fighting that separates them from other forces.

unusual sounds. This is traditionally down to the lead scout, or point man, in the patrol. He'll need to periodically listen for any sounds that are not native to the environment. (Before deployment, the team will have been listening to the sounds of native animals and birds to the region, so they can correctly identify them while on patrol.) A giveaway sound might only be distant and last for a second or two. Perhaps it's the faint but sharp crackling of a fire of an enemy patrol resting up, or the dull sound of boots trampling on leaves and twigs.

NAVIGATION

For most SF missions, the terrain the guys have to cross is unlikely to be free of pitfalls and obstacles. It would be great if they had to tab through dense dry forest for three days without any interruptions, but most combat zones take place in areas that are crawling with both natural and man-made obstacles, and the team will need to negotiate them each carefully.

NATURAL // Rivers can be difficult to cross, especially if it's deep, wide or fast-flowing. If the river is too cold the SF team will look to avoid crossing it: cold feet equals cramp and trench foot and an unnecessary extra problem for the team to deal with. If it can be crossed (the decision is down to the patrol scout), then they will cross in single file. For deeper rivers, the team will use what's known as a single rope bridge. First of all, the team selects a point on the bank to cross over. Then two guys will swim over to the other side and set up an anchor point. The patrol can then either crawl on top of the rope or hanging below it or rappel across.

The other way of crossing rivers is for the team to fill their Bergens with as much gear as possible, clip weapons to the Bergens using carabiners, and then tie them together using parachute cord. With one guy on each corner of the Bergens the team then enters the river at a bend, paying close attention to the direction of the current. You need to swim in the same direction as the current, using your survival belt as a floating mechanism. When the team reaches the other side of the bank three men will stay in the water with the Bergens while the fourth unclips his gun and makes sure the other side of the bank is clear. When crossing European rivers, which are colder than South American ones, it's advisable for the team to strip off its regular clothes and switch to waterproof Gore-Tex. When crossing jungle rivers, they're usually shallow and warm enough to just walk straight through.

Crossing a deep river is a very slow, time-consuming process, but it's important to do it properly, making sure that as much kit is waterproofed as possible, and changing out of your dry kit. I've crossed the Rhine before: it's absolutely bloody freezing, and believe me you need to have a dry kit to change into once you're out of the river. Otherwise you could get ill very fast.

Other natural obstacles such as open ground, hedges and gaps should be crossed as quickly as possible as the guys will be in a state of increased visibility to any nearby enemy troops. Finding the narrowest point to cross is vital.

MAN-MADE // Crossing man-made obstacles such as roads requires the team to use a patrol scout to carry out a recce of the surrounding area. In a hostile environment these areas are likely to be swarming with enemy activity and teams need to have full awareness of traffic density, frequency of police and military vehicles, locations of checkpoints and security cameras – anything that could potentially compromise the team's security and the mission. Taking all those factors into account they will then pick a time when it is less likely to be busy and at a point along the road where traffic jams are less frequent. In some Third World urban environments, where pollution creates a thick fog at certain hours of the day, the team will wait until the fog arrives and then cross. Minimising their visibility is key.

Gates and fences should be crawled under if possible, or vaulted, rather than opened. If they're locked and then breached, that will leave a clear marker for any potential tracker forces. Walls should be climbed over, with two men working together, one lifting the other up and rolling over the top, with the operator keeping himself flat so as not to create a sharp outline against the wall to any enemy scouts.

If a team has to cross a border or breach a perimeter they might need to get through concertina wire fences. Some people will tell you that crawling through them is possible using your rifle, but that's a risky manoeuvre – if the wire is too tense then it will spring back when pushed apart. Instead, most patrols will carry wire-cutters for this purpose. Improvised ladders can be laid over the wire to provide a safe crossing, and Bangalore torpedoes can also be used to blow a path through wire defences. Bangalore torpedoes are metal tubes that are joined together and filled with explosive material. Detonating the Bangalore creates an explosion of a radius of 3-4m.

SETTING UP CACHES

Ten days on foot is about the maximum an SF patrol can last without resupply. In situations when air support is provided the team will be resupplied by HALO drops, but in operations behind enemy lines, they will use caches. Caching is the art of securely storing weapons and supplies for future recovery.

They can be laid by a previous patrol for the SF team to collect, or the SF unit can plant the cache themselves upon insertion and dump a load of gear in it that they might only need during the exfiltration phase, meaning they don't have to carry an extremely heavy load in the initial phases of the mission. Caches can be for food, water, or weapons and ammunition.

When selecting a cache, operators must take into account several factors:

★ Is the site accessible, not only for placing weapons, but also for recovering them?

★ What is the anticipated enemy activity in the area surrounding the cache?

★ Is the cache area being used for other friendly activity (e.g. drop zones or safe houses)?

★ How far is the cache from the patrol's operations? They don't want to be travelling a long distance to recover the cache.

Cache sites can be concealed from the enemy by using natural foliage and scenery to camouflage them. They can also be buried, which is a much more secure method of storing equipment. If the team is operating in the vicinity of a river they might consider submerging the cache, but only if they are confident the equipment can be effectively waterproofed and won't be carried away by fast currents. Buried caches must be marked in a way that is visible to the SF team but invisible to the enemy – a small rock or a branch with its butt placed at the cache point, for example. Caves, caverns, loose bricks in walls, abandoned buildings, sewers and cable conduits can all also make extremely good cache sites. During the concealment phase two members of the patrol should set up the cache with the other two surveying the surrounding area. If the enemy is watching they may try and booby-trap the cache site once the SF patrol has moved on. If the patrol is planting a cache to leave for a later SF team they should try and make a sketch of the area. Trying to locate an area of soil or foliage on purely verbal instructions is time-consuming and can lead to confusion, whereas a sketch clearly demarcates the cache area for the recovery team. When the patrol goes to recover the cache they should beforehand perform a detailed recce of the surrounding area, again looking for any enemy activity, and also closely observe the cache site, looking for any obvious signs of tampering, such as distributed soil or crushed foliage, before carefully retrieving the cache items.

PATROL HARBOURS

In certain missions the team will have to conduct a variety of operations in a concentrated location. Under this scenario the guys might set up a patrol harbour and go into what's known as a harbour routine. They also serve as good tactical resupply points for smaller patrols out in the field. A harbour patrol requires several four-man patrols in order to function correctly.

In fading daylight the team will select an area that has some form of cover and line their vehicles up in a circle pointing out. The vehicles will then be decked out in camo cover to hide them from enemy airplanes and satellites. As night approaches the team will have guys stagging in the area surrounding the deconfliction zone, recceing the site. They will also get on the radio waves to make sure all friendly forces are aware of the coordinates of the deconfliction zone, especially aircraft, so the chances of a blue-on-blue are minimised.

The guys will then set up a HQ, from where the commander will run operations, aided by his signaller, a runner, a 2IC and a couple of guys on mortar duty. Set up in a circular perimeter around the HQ are sentry positions that are manned with GPMGs and sniper positions, and outside of this is a field of tripwired Claymores for extra protection. Depending on available manpower, some of the lads will also go out on clearing patrols outside of the patrol harbour to check on any nearby enemy activity, and also to go further afield to collect resupplies.

Patrol harbours are vital for the handover of prisoners and intelligence. They also provide a welcome relief for SF patrols on long, hard tabs. At a resupply point a knackered four-man patrol can refuel, stock up on supplies, have a scoff and perhaps even shower in a 45-gallon drum.

AVOIDING TRACKERS

Tracking and counter-tracking are two sides of the same coin. If you're good at one, you're probably good at the other as well. Counter-tracking is an essential part of any SF team's capability, because it allows the team to remain undetected even when they've got the enemy on their backs.

Human beings, depending on how careless they are, will nearly always leave some evidence of their existence in an area, whether they were just passing through or settling down for a quick scoff and couple of hours' kip. Whilst it's helpful for the operator to identify those signs and build up as complete a picture as possible of the enemy from small and seemingly insignificant details, it's doubly important to mission success that they don't repeat the same mistakes as their opponents.

There are some simple precautions soldiers can take to reduce the chances of detection. Remember, the guys tracking the SF patrol are probably not mugs. Trackers might also be natives who have lived in the surrounding environment all their lives, and can read signs as well as or even better than the SF team, because of their natural familiarity. In Vietnam, VC trackers were adept at noticing even the smallest detail to indicate that US troops had recently passed through and were nearby, allowing them to launch surprise ambushes on the unsuspecting troopers. So it pays to be careful.

Troops carrying a heavy load must be careful when travelling through forests and shrubbery – their backpacks could easily nick against bark and leave a tell-tale scratch, or snap a weak branch – a dead giveaway.

Operators pay special attention to the way they walk. Stones and leaves can reveal a soldier's presence, as leaves rot on the underside and stones create depressions in the ground, so displacement of either object is immediately noticeable to the skilled tracker. The guys must take care not to kick any ground material out of position as they walk.

Footprints are the most visible sign of human activity. If a tracker comes across a series of footprints, they've really hit the jackpot.

From a simple set of prints, the skilled tracker can deduce a whole load of information. For example, lots of crushed twigs or a wide area of flattened grass means there is large troop movement. Trackers can also establish the size of a group by identifying the footprints of the rear soldier in the group (his prints will be the freshest and clearest) and then counting the number of prints and faded prints between a first and second stride of the key print. The number of prints will indicate the size of the patrol. Age of the prints can also be determined by other factors. For example, prints whose depressions are filled with water are likely to have been made before the most recent bout of rainfall. The load of a unit or operator can also be estimated by the depth of the footprint

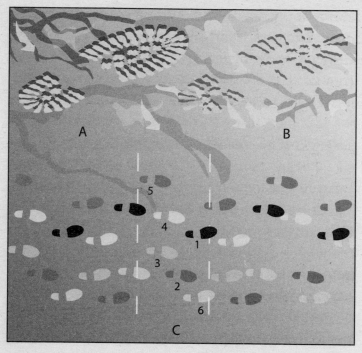

Footprints are the most obvious sign of recent human activity in an area. Interpreted correctly they can provide a ream of information. A tracker can tell that print A is more recent than print B because it's a more distinct print – over time the soil hardens and dries and the print breaks down. Multiple sets of prints as seen in C can also be interpreted for enemy strength. A tracker identifies the footprints of the rear soldier in the group (his prints will be the freshest and clearest) and then counting the number of prints and faded prints between a first and second stride of the key print. Here there are 6 separate sets of prints.

impression. Enemy fitness and morale can also be ascertained from footprints – if the team is struggling to maintain a certain pace, or are depressed by their combat conditions, they will have less time or make less effort to effectively cover their tracks.

Taking simple, effective precautions such as making sure the guys take all their food and body waste with them, reapplying camo paint to ensure they remain less visible, and avoiding patrolling across areas with long grass, can help operators stay covert and avoid costly enemy encounters that could reduce the team's fighting numbers. Operators also have to be aware of generating noise and should be trained in the process of silent routine: using field signals instead of speaking, and only whispering when absolutely necessary. They should also make sure to avoid making a noise when cleaning kit and having a scoff.

Covering footprints should also be practised by using leafy branches to wipe over the tracks and then laying twigs and leaves on top of the branch marks. This is a painstaking process, however, and not really ideal especially if the team is hard pressed to arrive at a destination by a certain time. The SF unit might also decide to employ false trail techniques, such as zig-zagging rather than walking in straight lines, to try

Counter-tracking requires discipline, focus and attention to detail. When you're in a hostile environment, you can feel nervous and on edge, and your natural instinct is to reach your mission objectives as quickly as possible and get the hell out. Being a Special Forces professional is all about curbing those instincts and relying on your training and intelligence to keep you alive.

and throw the enemy. As I mentioned earlier, walking in loops is time-consuming and when the operators are exhausted and hungry and tired it can be tempting to cut corners, but this is a highly effective method of staying ahead of trackers.

If the team knows it is being followed and it is only a matter of time before they are attacked by the enemy, they might decide to lay Claymore mines at chosen intervals as they move on. Claymores are perfect for ambushes, or for covering a team's flanks or escape route. The great thing about Claymores is that they can be set up individually, or wired together and set off with an M57 firing device commonly known as a clacker. Used simultaneously, the Claymore will blanket a 60° area in front of it in overlapping arcs of steel ball shrapnel and create a lethal killing zone of around 100 yards. Claymores can also be set to detonate using a time-delayed firing fuse. Claymore mines are a great deterrent — set a few of these off and the enemy is likely to think twice about pursuing you.

ENEMY CONTACT

The SF team's first aim should always be to complete the mission without any distractions. A recce mission completed without a shot fired is a successful one. But in tighter environments, or densely populated terrain, the patrol will only be able to avoid enemy detection for so long, and the chances of being sucked into a gunfight increase the longer the team is out there in the field. That's why it's important the team is prepared for encountering enemy forces of all sizes and strengths, and operators put in hard shifts on the training ground practising drills for precisely these types of encounter.

If the patrol makes visual contact with the enemy, the team leader must decide whether to engage. He'll make the call based on several factors, including how it impacts on the team's overall mission, and also taking into account the size of the enemy force. Sometimes this is decided at the mission planning stage. Orders are given by the military chiefs as to whether the patrol has permission to engage enemy forces. The rules of war are complicated and there are sometimes very detailed sets of criteria dictating when a team is allowed to open fire.

But of course, sometimes there's no time to make these decisions, or the enemy makes visual contact first and opens fire. In these situations, the team will use contact drill techniques to deal with the threat.

Once contact is inevitable, the SF team reacts swiftly. And that doesn't mean having an eight-hour firefight in the middle of a clearing. Extended battles between the SF patrol and the enemy are a bad idea. As the battle is happening behind enemy lines, the bad guys can call in for plenty of reinforcements, whilst the SF team are on their own. Sooner or later, the overwhelming numbers they are up against will put them in extreme danger of capture or death. Long gun battles also deplete a soldier's ammunition reserves, and it's vital to conserve rounds, especially if resupplies are out of the question. The name of the game is to keep the enemy distant, and disappear back into hidden terrain, with as few spent rounds and injured soldiers as possible. Shoot and scoot – keep it stupid-simple.

Surprise contacts require speed of thought and movement, and the patrol operating in a coordinated, tactical manner. And that's why patrol formation and routine is so important.

FORMATION // There are several formations open to a Special Forces patrol, depending on the type of terrain they are moving in, the number of men in the patrol and the enemy they are facing – guerrilla or traditional armed forces. There are four main formations used by SF patrols:

LINE // (–) Along with file, the most basic patrol formation. Great for providing good firepower to the front and rear, not very good for the flanks if the team is attacked to the left or right.

FILE // (I) The file formation is ideal for patrols in situations when the team must negotiate narrow paths or routes and expects little or no enemy contact. The lead scout sits at the top of the file, with the patrol commander behind him. The lead scout's job is to stay alert and look out for anything amiss or out of the ordinary – mines, booby traps, enemy contacts. Lead scouts have to have eyes like shit-house rats and mustn't miss a thing. To his immediate six is the patrol commander, who directs the mission and decides on the patrol formation. Behind him the rest of the patrol looks left and right, scanning the flanks for potential threats, whilst a tail-end Charlie (TEC) brings up the rear.

WEDGE // (^) The Americans call this the Arrowhead. There's one big difference between the Yanks' and the Regiment's use of this system – in

American teams the Patrol Commander sits at the front of the arrow, whereas in the SAS formation the lead scout takes up the arrowhead point, with the patrol commander positioned behind. This is a good formation to use if the team is expecting, but not certain of, attack.

ECHELON // (/, \ ) good if the team is expecting an attack on one side but not the other. In the echelon formation the team is arranged on angle to the left or right of the lead scout. The disadvantage to the echelon formation is that the opposite flank of the attack is left exposed.

In all patrols the team is silent at all times and communicates with hand signals and gestures. It's up to the whole team to remain totally alert and maintain battle focus. Because when the crap hits the fan, the situation can deteriorate quickly unless the team is sharp and responds rapidly.

In a jungle patrol the team should plan for surprise contacts by moving in single file, with the lead scout armed with a shotgun. Checking his compass, the lead scout will also look for tracks, smells, any sign at all of human activity or tampering. Periodically he will

It's important for the lead scout in a patrol to rotate in order to stay fresh and alert. One trait that is appreciated in the SAS is honesty – if a soldier's knackered and can't concentrate he needs to say so. It's no good doing the job half-cocked and risking the security of the patrol because he's too tough to admit he's shattered.

stop and assess movement or a sound up ahead. Patrol movement can be painfully slow, but it pays to be careful.

In the event that a team does run into the enemy, they will go into contact mode. The lead scout will initiate the contact by moving forward and putting rounds down. Meanwhile the rest of the team will shout 'break left' or 'break right', moving to cover either side of the lead scout. The important thing for Special Forces patrols is to be able to think on their feet, as both individuals and a unit. You have to be flexible on the ground, so if the terrain is not suited to breaking right, you don't break right, no matter how many times you've practised that in training. Similarly if there is a ridge then the team needs to split up into two smaller teams. The structure has to be fluid, not fixed, and you have to have soldiers who can think on their feet, in the middle of an intense, seemingly chaotic firefight.

The team will then look to establish a baseline using the Fire and Movement technique. This could be in a ditch or a dip in the ground, although the team should be aware that some baselines are booby-trapped, as some of the lads have found out to their cost in Afghanistan. Once the baseline has been

The principle behind Fire and Movement (F&M) tactics is that teams operate in two-man firing squads, with one guy putting rounds down whilst the other moves. It's vital that one guy moves only whilst the other is providing covering fire. When moving, operators will generally stick to 10m increments so as not to put too much distance between themselves and their firing partner. Moving in bounds, the guys will look to close in on the enemy until they have gained the initiative. In F&M tactics it's also vital that the guys communicate using hand signals and verbal commands. When one guy empties his mag or suffers a stoppage, the other guy has to be ready to put rounds down straight away, to keep the enemy pinned down.

established the patrol members will pepper-pot back to break left or right out of the contact, two men laying down fire whilst the other two retreat to the baseline.

In a man down situation, where one of the patrol guys is injured inside the contact zone, two guys will have to go in to grab the stricken soldier. They will establish a baseline and one of the guys will put down suppressing fire whilst the other goes in to fetch the man down. He will then pepper-pot back to the baseline, using available cover to shield his retreat and protect the wounded soldier.

If the contact is to the flanks then the team will need to charge the enemy using the advance-to-contact drill, with the patrol advancing by taking turns in small teams to go firm and lay down fire, and advance towards the contact.

ENEMY AMBUSHES

In Afghanistan, elite teams have to contend with ambush traps set by al-Qaeda/Taleban (AQT) fighters. In the perfect trap, the AQT launch an ambush against the operators, then quickly withdraw down a valley or ridge. The team then moves forward to

Nothing can prepare you for the sheer intensity of a firefight. And SF soldiers need to be able to remain calm under pressure and think tactically in heated gun battles. In the US, soldiers are taught to stick to a pre-planned routine in the event of a contact. I don't agree with that. Operators should be able to think on their feet and respond to the situation in front of them.

counter-attack the AQT combatants. As they close in, they are attacked on both flanks from hidden AQT teams waiting in ambush mode. Another technique relies on the covert abilities of the enemy forces. When they spy an SF team they enter stealth mode, hiding from view and observing the elite operators. They are waiting for the guys to take up Observation Posts (OPs) when surveying the target or the approach area. When the team has moved on, the enemy sets up elaborate booby traps at each of the SF's OPs. When the SF team makes its return patrol and heads for the same OPs, the traps are activated and the soldiers incinerated. These types of ambush technique have been in use since the days of the Native Americans against the US cavalry, but they are still highly effective at inflicting casualties on the SF team and damaging morale. It's vital for the team to take precautions when operating in hostile environments – making sure they tab in loops, calculating whether a contact is designed to lead them into a flanking manoeuvre trap, or ensuring that the team doesn't get lazy and use the same OPs more than once.

RV TACTICS

In hectic combat scenarios, operators can become detached from the rest of their unit. When this happens, the patrol members will stick to a pre-arranged plan of heading to a series of designated RV points in order to regroup:

EMERGENCY RV // This is set every 200 metres during a patrol. If things get messy, you would go there and wait fifteen minutes. It's essentially a close rallying point, but once the time is up, you need to move on.

PATROL RV // This is where you would go next and here wait for up to 24 hours. If you didn't link up with anyone after that point, then you would move on again.

WAR RV // The closest available security force location, this is a pre-designated position that the team will head to when all else fails. In the Gulf War, our War RV was in Syria.

SPECIAL TERRAIN TACTICS

The above patrol and combat tactics are capable of being used in pretty much any environment or terrain. But extreme terrains can present very different challenges to Special Forces patrols, and they need to adapt their tactics accordingly. In the Regiment, each

Troop specialises in certain extreme terrain and environments – although every operator should be prepared to deal with any conditions thrown at them.

Mobility Troop's traditional area of operation has been the desert. The incredibly high temperatures and lack of water are a logistical nightmare when it comes to planning patrols, and to make matters worse, desert temperatures can plummet dramatically during night-time. I should know that better than anyone else – in the Iraqi desert, we found ourselves sweating buckets during the day, but after dusk our kit was too thin to keep us warm. You are fighting a constant battle against sunstroke and dehydration. Sunstroke in particular can be fatal. This is when the body overheats by absorbing more heat than it can get rid of by sweating, and can lead to a coma if untreated. In this situation the lads will take off the guy's clothes, find some shade (if they're in the desert and none is present they will dig a shallow hide to create some) and drip cool water over his body in an attempt to cool him down. This is only a temporary fix though; if a guy in a patrol is down with sunstroke he will in all likelihood need to be medevacced.

Carrying enough water also presents a real difficulty for long-range patrols. A lack of water can play havoc with the mind, creating illusions such as the famous 'oasis' mirages. Take it from me, these are real problems for anyone enduring a long-range desert patrol, and it requires extreme mental toughness and focus to be able to tell the difference between reality and illusion when you are in a starved, dehydrated, exhausted state. Other extreme weather fronts, such as sandstorms and flash floods, risk-turning even the best prepared mission into a disaster.

Mobility Troop's rule of thumb for desert movement is only move during the night if you have to, when it's cooler. The added benefit of moving at night is that, if the temperature does drop extremely low, tabbing at least warms up the body and stops joints from freezing.

Avoiding detection in the desert is more difficult, because there aren't really the mountains, hills and dead ground (i.e. gullies and stream beds) that are natural to other terrains. The desert is like one giant clearing. The desert's long, open, inhospitable terrain does come with one big advantage: the enemy's lines of communication and patrol will be few and far between, often using the one or two motorways that pass through the desert. This makes it much easier for the team to observe enemy activity.

The guys in the SAS's Mobility Troop are experts at desert warfare. They spend as much time as possible in the desert. This means they are supremely conditioned for the tough conditions of the desert and need less time to acclimatise than Special Forces teams unfamiliar with the harsh desert environment.

Some of the SAS's first missions were fought in the sweltering hot jungles of Malaya in the years after the Second World War. The Regiment's performance in an inhospitable jungle environment generated huge respect in Whitehall and helped forge their reputation as an elite fighting unit. It was here that they developed many of the essential fighting techniques of jungle and swamp warfare, and sharpened them in Borneo in the 1960s during the Indonesia-Malayan confrontation, penetrating the Indonesian border to launch deep raids behind enemy lines.

When patrolling in the jungle, operators have to be prepared to cope with reduced visibility. Dark and difficult to navigate through, humidity is also a real problem. Even in dry seasons the jungle is damp and uncomfortable, and the moist, warm conditions are a breeding ground for parasites and diseases as well as indigenous creatures such as snakes. Trees are everywhere, and it only takes one guy to leave a single mark for expert indigenous trackers to start breathing down their neck. Operators have to pay particular attention to:

BRANCHES AND BARK // As I said earlier, protruding rifle ends or gear from backpacks can nick against tree bark, leaving a fresh scar. Branches can be snapped as operators move through tight areas. Operators must pay attention to their field of vision and watch out for branches.

GRASS // Some grass, such as savannah grass, is especially tall and when trampled on leaves clear evidence of their movement. Tall grass should be avoided if at all possible.

LEAVES AND TWIGS // Rotten leaves and twigs litter the undergrowth of jungle canopies. Twigs can snap easily underfoot, and walking over leaves can overturn them, exposing the different-coloured underside.

BUSHES AND PLANTS // Some of these have thorns that can snare on an operator's clothing or backpack, tearing off small patches.

SWAMP AND MARSH LAND // This type of terrain is damp and the boot of an operator will sink deeply in, leaving footprints that will remain there for longer than a footprint impression made in dry soil. In addition, the wet puddles natural to swamp and marsh land can splash onto surrounding rocks, grass and leaves. The guys must pay attention to the undergrowth and avoid ground which is overly soft or wet.

Tribesmen can play a vital role in Special Forces operations. When the SAS was deployed to Borneo in 1962, the Regiment boys used local tribesmen to supervise vast areas of jungle, tracking signs of Indonesian activity. Less than 100 men were deployed along a border measuring more than 1,500km in length. It would have been all but impossible to accurately track the Indonesians across such a vast area of jungle – but thanks to the help of the tribesmen, the SAS could still operate effectively.

The Black Hawk helicopter can fit 16 guys on board. It's one of the best troop-carrying birds out there and has seen extensive use in South America, Iraq and Afghanistan. You can abseil or fast-rope from them and they are also good attack support birds too, as two mounted mini-guns can provide suppressive fire for ground troops, as well as establishing clearing areas in hostile territory. In Somalia, local gangsters called 'Skinnies' targeted Black Hawks using RPGs. These bastards would use the RPG's self detonating mechanism (RPGs self-destruct after being airborne at distances over 900m) to knock down the helicopters. At one point in the skies over Mogadishu, some 200 RPGs were in the air.

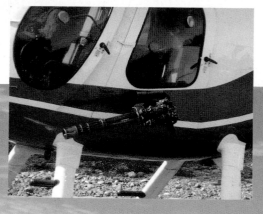

The Little Bird can turn on a six-pence and take out targets using a mini-gun that has a phenomenal rate of fire.

The Huey (or the UH1-Iroquois as it's formally known) was used extensively in Vietnam and has developed a reputation as a great workhorse. It's very reliable, a good troop transporter and can take a rocket and still function. The Huey can just go and go and go.

Right: Helicopters can also be useful for operators providing precision fire to ground forces, such as this sniper from Brazil's BOPE unit. Tied to a lanyard, with his feet resting on the rail, the guy will use his weapon to pick off targets from above. His privileged aerial view enables him to engage enemy forces that might not be visible to the lads on the ground.

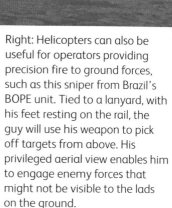

Helicopters are capable of carrying out extractions from small locations where it would be impossible to land an airplane, or on artificial platforms constructed from timber and gravel.

Air insertion is a powerful way for Special Forces operators to go to war.

Right: The AC-130 Gunship was introduced in Vietnam. This is an aircraft that has serious firepower – 4 x 7.62mm miniguns, 20mm Vulcan cannons and in some versions a 105mm M102 Howitzer.

US Special Forces operators being extracted by Black Hawk helicopter, harnessed to a single rope hanging from the aircraft.

Above: The Skulls used by BOPE for manoeuvring around the violent favelas of Rio de Janeiro. Unlike modern urban warfare vehicles these Skulls aren't fitted with run flat tyres (which anchor the tyre beads to the rim flange of the wheel, keeping the tyre operation even when flat). Run flat tyres can take a 7.62mm round and still go at 30mph. Without these tyres, all it takes is a single round and the BOPE guys have to get out in a hostile environment and manually change the tyres. The joke amongst BOPE operators is that they can change a tyre quicker than a Ferrari pit-stop crew!

A minefield in the Falklands, a legacy of the 1982 war.

Special combat rebreather systems recirculate air, preventing bubbles from disclosing the operator's location.

APS Underwater Rifle.

Below: Combat divers from the US Special Forces Group linking up with a submarine in preparation for an insertion closer to their mission objective.

Ghillie suit helmets as worn by the Sri Lankan Special Task Force for camouflage. A full Ghillie suit is too heavy to wear on patrol but snipers will wear a full one when taking up a firing position.

Jungle rivers are shallow enough to walk through.

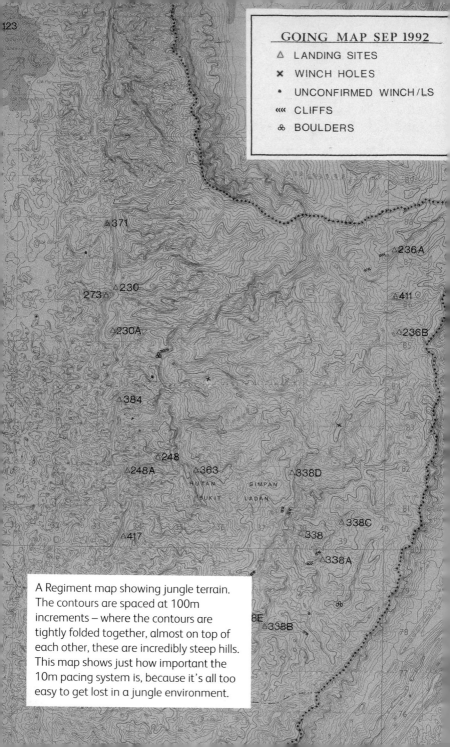

123

△ 371

△ 236A

△ 230
273 △

△ 411

△ 230A

△ 236B

△ 384

△ 248
△ 248A   △ 363   △ 338D

HUTAN   SIMPAN
BUKIT   LADAN

△ 338C

△ 417

△ 338

△ 338A

8E △ 338B

A Regiment map showing jungle terrain.
The contours are spaced at 100m
increments – where the contours are
tightly folded together, almost on top of
each other, these are incredibly steep hills.
This map shows just how important the
10m pacing system is, because it's all too
easy to get lost in a jungle environment.

Jungle terrain is an enemy tracker's wet dream and causes serious logistical problems for even the most experienced Special Forces operators. The best way of learning the ins and outs of the jungle and navigating effectively is for the team to use the specialist indigenous knowledge of the jungle tribes.

When I was in the SAS I was in Mountain Troop. Arctic and mountain warfare and survival was our key skill.

Moving in a snowy, icy terrain is awkward and time-consuming. Forget using vehicles — nothing beats good old skis for easy, quick movement. Skis are a great way of moving rapidly across exposed land, and also for launching raids or escaping enemy contact.

Snowshoes are slower and a bit more energy-sapping, but they're also a good way of negotiating arctic terrain and better suited to areas where the snow is loose. Snowshoes might seem like an old-fashioned concept but again it's all about keeping it stupid-simple. There's no reason to rely on special snow vehicles when a decent pair of snowshoes can get you from A to B. Special Forces teams have to learn to overlap the inner edges of their snowshoes. If they tried walking normally they'd develop 'straddle-gait'

which would leave them exhausted and even lead to serious injury. Although modern snowshoes use advanced design and materials to increase the soldier's weight distribution, they still leave a slight impression in the snow, and the lead scout (known as the 'trailbreaker') will have to exert more energy than the other guys in the patrol because he will be lifting his snowshoes through fresh snow, whereas the other guys in the patrol can follow the footstep impressions he has already made. It's important for the guys to keep their feet parallel to the ground as they lift them up – when we walk normally, we tend to lift the foot forward and up in an angular motion. In the arctic, that would quickly exhaust the lads as their feet would be constantly having to swing through snow with each step forward, rather than plunging into it in a downward motion that requires less force.

Teams will use specialised kit for arctic missions – for example, wearing white camo kits rather than digi-cam to help them blend into the natural environment more effectively.

The arctic environment also affects the kind of mission the patrol team is capable of carrying out. Long-range recce missions are more difficult because the team has only a limited supply of heat and insulated clothing. Launching attacks is slow so the team is more likely to carry out an assault in support of air strikes, or even call in the air strikes themselves on a designated target. As with the desert, arctic terrain is likely to have a very low population density and only a limited infrastructure. This means that knocking out a supply depot or radar installation is likely to cause major disruption to enemy activity. The team also has a tough task on its hands when it comes to counter-tracking, because every footstep leaves a deep impression in the snow. This can be partially avoided by sticking to skis instead of snowshoes. But rather than attempting to cover up its own tracks, the team can actively send confusing messages to any trackers by leaving fake ski or snowshoe tracks behind. These can be laid along trails that lead to booby traps, or positioning snipers to the rear of the group to pick off any lone trackers, although this measure should only be done when the team knows it's being followed and needs to take rapid action to allow it to continue the mission. If you kill someone behind you, the bad guys up ahead are likely to hear about it sooner rather than later.

It's vital for the patrol to set up shelters in the snow that can protect the guys from the outside elements. Although arctic environments have very low

Hypothermia is a real threat to operators in arctic environments. Once I was dropped off in Siberia and the temperature fell from -29°C to -46°C. After three days I was suffering from frostbite and hypothermia and I was minutes from dying. My mind was spinning; I was so far gone that even reading my GPS navigator was beyond me. In my hypothermic state, suffering hallucinations, I had convinced myself that the RV was located in a gap in a pine forest situated about a mile away. Luckily I avoided stumbling towards the gap in the pine forest – but if I had acted on my thoughts I would have ended up a dead man.

temperatures, snow is in fact a good insulator and building a snow shelter can provide the unit with somewhere warm using their body heat or a small fire. But building snow shelters is also a race against time, before the guys freeze to death. Teams can construct rapid shelters by making a mound from foliage, covering it with a poncho sheet, and then heaping a thick layer of snow on top. After 30 minutes the outer layer will have frozen and the team can make a tunnel and excavate the foliage from inside. Another fast way of making a shelter is to locate some spruce trees (the ones that look like Christmas trees) as these often have a clear space at the trunk. Here the guys can dig out the snow and use this as a temporary shelter, using the lower branches for bedding. Fires in arctic shelters don't have to be big – just one candle can increase the temperature in a sealed snow shelter by several degrees.

Mountain Troop students undertake intensive training in both arctic and mountain warfare and patrol because wherever you get snow you're probably going to find mountains, and vice versa. The wide nature of Mountain Troop's training skills means they can fight in a huge variety of combat zones, from the freezing peaks of Scandinavia down to the bare, dusty mountains of Afghanistan. In fact some of the ex-

Regiment lads have even gone on to scale Everest. During Mountain Troop training they will work on all aspects of mountaineering, from ice-climbing to fixed roping, mountain rescue and even working with avalanche dogs during search and rescue missions. Believe me, there's nothing as hardcore as training for special ops at high altitude.

There are some ground rules for climbing mountains. Before beginning the ascent, the operator needs to be equipped with the right gear. He'll need specially modified climbing shoes equipped with rubber soles that 'stick' to rock faces for extra grip and balance. Climbing harnesses are required to secure the climber to a piece of rope or anchor. Sit-string, chest or full-body harnesses are used, depending on the terrain and the load the guy is carrying. Carabiners are used for latching on to rope lines, and nuts for securing the lines.

There are usually two lead scouts in a mountain patrol, and these are the guys who have more mountain experience than the rest of the troop (as arctic and mountain warfare is usually practised by the same team, there will always be one or two guys who are more advanced climbers). Their job is to prepare for an ascent for the other members of the team to follow them. The lead climbers will set up what's known as an A-frame — two similarly sized beams, arranged in a 45-degree or greater angle, attached to a horizontal beam lying on top. This gives the lead climbers a bit of extra height allowing them to fix in place bolted ropes, suspension traverses and vertical hauling lines to aid the ascent.

When climbing a mountain, the first rule of thumb is: don't try and climb over obstacles. Instead climb *around* them. That way, you avoid getting in a fix with no way out.

There are several common techniques used to negotiate mountains:

LEAD CLIMBING // is where the lead climber is attached to a climbing rope and the second lead climber acts as a belayer, who is anchored into the rock face for security. He holds the rope and applies friction to it in case of a fall. The belayer is also used to control the descent of heavy loads down the mountain face.

MANTLING // a specific rock-climbing technique for climbing onto ledges. This needs serious upper body strength, particularly in the shoulders, lats and back, as well as solid wrist grip. The climber puts both hands on the ledge and lifts himself up until his head is above his hands. At this point the climber operator is no longer pulling up, but pushing down with his hands. Rotating his palms to make his grip on the ledge more secure, he then raises a foot onto the ledge and transfers his body weight onto it to even out the balance. He can then free his hands and use them to grip holds in the wall facing the ledge, and hoist up his other leg.

STEMMING // is the art of using opposing forces to allow the operator to climb up 'chimneys' (parallel cracks about a foot or so apart from each other) or in situations where two walls meet at an angle. By pressing his feet and hands into the opposite sides of the crack or section, the soldier can hold his weight and shift himself slowly up. This is also a good technique for pushing off a lower hold and onto a hold placed higher up.

Going down is much trickier than climbing up; the difficulty depends on the gradient of the cliff face, the steeper it is: the harder the task facing the operator, because the footholds become all but invisible and make the climb-down treacherous. On the steepest descents one of the lead scouts will try to secure a vantage point to pinpoint footholds and fissures and relay that information to the guy making the initial descent. He will then have clear instructions on where to place his feet. On nearly all mountain descents teams will use ropes to abseil down. Only in extreme situations will they consider going down without a rope. For example, if the team is being pursued and needs to make a hasty exit, they will make a ropeless descent. But this is a high-risk activity and should only be practised by climbers with lots of mountain experience.

URBAN WARFARE

Fighting in built-up areas can be extremely hazardous. Built-up urban environments are difficult to tactically manoeuvre through. In a city like Baghdad or the favelas of Rio de Janeiro, the streets are narrow, dark alleyways are everywhere and buildings can house snipers. Patrols often have to go it alone in urban warfare – armoured personnel carriers are hugely restricted in their movement. In Brazil, the Skulls BOPE use to navigate around the favelas often encounter home-made roadblocks in the roads which the guys have to then clear out before resuming the mission – creating a delay and making the team sitting ducks for any snipers. Helicopters and other support vehicles are also at danger from RPG attacks.

233

Urban warfare is nerve-jangling even for experienced operators as you're never sure where the next threat is coming from, particularly if the civilian population is also hostile. In Iraq, the psychological and physical stress on the soldiers can be huge.

House and street clearances are a vital aspect of urban warfare for elite operators. The guys will have to check streets for threats but will stick to the shaded, narrow areas of the street – in the open they'd be an easy target for enemy fighters. The guys perform thorough checks on rooftops to check for rogue snipers, houses, gardens and even the sewer systems. During house clearances the team will establish a base, which is usually the first house they have cleared. The guys will use this house as a reference point when clearing out each further house. Houses should ideally be cleared from the top down, and it should be a very thorough search – even cellars and outhouses have to be checked for any threats. These can be stressful situations as the guys will have families screaming and terrified civilians all over the shop, but it's important to keep their minds focused on the job.

Special attention has to be paid to the weapons used in house clearances. When dealing with pre-fab homes or old structures, using explosive weapons in such a weak building can cause floors and roofs to cave in and potentially injure the operator. Instead he'll stick to light machine guns and shotguns for solid firepower that carries a low risk of fatal structural damage.

235

Despite all the equipment that elite operators work with today, technology can, and does, break down. When I was posted in Iraq we had numerous hi-tech comms systems and radios and none of them worked. Some of them had the wrong frequency, there were bad connections with the satellite phone as it couldn't get aligned with the satellite. All that hi-tech kit and it ended up with me sending Morse code to Cyprus to get relayed to the Middle East.

06
OBSERVATION
AND
SURVEILLANCE

> ELITE OPERATORS ARE PAST MASTERS AT ESTABLISHING OPS AND CARRYING OUT RECCES //

And although nowadays armed forces have access to Predator drones, U2 spy planes, advanced SIGINT from orbiting satellites and electronic technology for mapping out enemy forces and terrain, gathering intelligence still remains a massively important part of the Regiment's business. That's because there's only so much a hi-tech satellite can tell military chiefs. To really understand the enemy, they're still going to need eyes and ears on the ground, monitoring the bad guys up close and personal. And that's where elite operators come in.

ESTABLISHING OBSERVATION POSTS

OPs have been used by Special Forces for years, and are still a key part of SF warfare today in Afghanistan and Iraq. Although satellite imagery can monitor enemy positions, the problem with technology is that there's always the possibility that it might break down, and you can never get a real feel of the situation. It's always better to have a Mark One Eyeball on the ground providing a running commentary of what the target is doing, what the weather and humidity is like, what approaches to the target exist, where an attack could be launched from, checking out the enemy morale and kit and routine to see how professional they are.

Special Forces teams are trained in establishing temporary OPs. They can be used for long-range surveillance, collecting data, verifying targets and gaining a more complete picture of the enemy from the ground, noting things that are more difficult to spot from the air such as the sudden increase in traffic volume on roads or railways, which could reveal the next planned offensive, or planes taking off from a runway for a bombing mission. This intelligence is vital in planning effective assaults. SF teams performing OPs can also call in air or artillery strikes on verified targets, a tactic that has been practised by Special Forces teams in Afghanistan.

Setting up an OP depends on several factors. How long is the team going to be there? What type of surveillance do they need to carry out? What's the terrain and weather like? Do they need to take extra precautions not to be seen? For example, guys on long-range patrols deep behind enemy lines don't want to stick around too long in any one place. To remain covert they must set up temporary OPs and then relocate, and repeat on a regular basis. If intelligence indicates that enemy missile launchers are being prepared to fire, then it's a race against time to sort an OP, establish the targets, identify the weak spots and call in the air strikes.

The priority is to make sure the OP blends in with the natural environment. It's no good carrying out surveillance if you're spotted. There's also got to be a clear line of sight to the target being watched. If the patrol can't properly see what's going on, they might miss crucial intelligence. If there are two or more OPs for the patrol then they need to be positioned closely enough to allow the teams to communicate with each other, facilitate the exchange of information and also rotate personnel. OPs should be constructed low to the ground and have an escape route should the team be compromised during the surveillance mission. In my experience, it's also helpful to construct an OP in a site where the enemy least expects it – so avoiding busy roads, railway tracks or hill crests that would silhouette the OP is essential. A less obvious OP – say, beneath some undergrowth or thick bushes – is a much better bet. And it should be near a water supply too, particularly if the team is going to be inhabiting the OP for weeks rather than days.

It's best to construct an OP at night, when enemy activity is likely to be minimal. That gives the team until sunrise to complete the OP. Working at speed but with care, the team will then dig a hide and cover it with camouflage and waterproofed material, making sure that any earth that has been disturbed is also camouflaged. It's critical that no signs of human activity are visible at the OP.

The team can choose from different types of OP. OPs on open ground are useful if the ground is too rocky or is frozen over and hard to dig a hide into. Foxholes, like those used by soldiers in the Second World War, are basic but can be set up quickly and are easily camouflaged. Then you get the more complex OPs built like tents or totally underground hides or bunkers. These take longer to build and need a good supply of local materials to construct – branches strong enough to create an overhead canopy to cover the tent or underground hide, for example. The team will also need to stop the underground hide from caving in and falling on top of the soldiers. Sandbags are a good, simple solution to this problem. Operators can carry empty sandbags, fill them with the dirt they dug up (which saves them the hassle of having to re-bury it elsewhere – remember, dug up earth is a different colour to topsoil and is a red flag to a beady enemy scout) and mould them into virtually any shape they need. Digging also takes up a lot of energy, so the ground has to be soft and fairly loose, otherwise the guys will have to bust a serious gut just to get the hide set up, and risk being too exhausted to properly clear up after themselves. The tent cover can be made from a poncho or the SF patrol might carry some plastic waterproof sheeting especially. Parachute suspension cord can be used as the frame for the hide cover.

OPs don't have to be in the middle of a woodland area or a field – they can be mobile too, such as the taxis used by elite operators on the streets of Baghdad to target high-ranking terrorist suspects. During the rescue of Norman Kember, James Loney and Harmeet Sooden in Baghdad in 2006, British SAS, in tandem with US and Canadian special forces, used taxis and civilian trucks to approach the house where the trio were being held. Making this type of false flag approach meant they could properly stag out the area before launching what was ultimately a highly successful assault, with all three guys rescued.

In house-clearance scenarios the guys will look to establish an OP in a nearby abandoned building or even the back of a van parked nearby, using electronic surveillance equipment to build up a picture of the target.

OPs can be constructed for either four-man or two-man patrols. In a four-man OP there's a sentry and radio operator on duty to perform the surveillance work. The other two guys will be resting and sleeping. The team rotates their roles at strict clockwork intervals. This is to keep everyone on their toes and make sure that no enemy activity goes unnoticed. It's hard to stay focused for more than a few hours at a time. On a two-man OP they go into hard routine mode with one man doing surveillance and radio work and the other sleeping, rotating every forty minutes to an hour – but any longer and the operator risks going into a deeper state of sleep called REM (rapid eye movement) sleep, which causes drowsiness when the sleeper awakes.

CALCULATING DISTANCES

Operators should be able to determine the approximate distance of enemy soldiers without any hi-tech gadgetry. They can do this by memorising some basic principles about visual detail and distance. For example, at a distance of 100m an enemy soldier's details will be clear and identifiable to the naked eye. At 300m, the colour of the enemy combatant's face will register, as will his outline, but subtler details such as his equipment will become hard to make out. At a range of 600m the operator will only be able to establish an indistinct body shape, with even the head not visible from this distance.

As a general rule, objects will appear deceptively close to the naked eye when they are higher up than the observer's position, when the object is significantly larger than the surrounding environment or when the area between the operator and the object is dead ground. The object might appear further away than it really is if the operator is carrying out his recce lying flat on the ground or when natural light and visibility are poor.

SCANNING TECHNIQUES

When carrying out OPs and recceing targets, operators need to be able to scan an area systematically in order to pick up objects of interest or unusual movements. They will do so by conducting a detailed scan of a given area. First they will divide the area to be scanned into foreground (closest area), middle ground and distance (the area furthest away). Starting with the foreground the operator will move his eyes horizontally in short, overlapping movements. He will repeat the process for the middle ground and distance.

SPECIAL SURVEILLANCE TECHNIQUES

Observing enemy targets is about more than just using your eyes and ears. In the hi-tech world of modern elite combat, electronic surveillance measures are just as important to a mission. Special Forces operators are trained in the use of a variety of top-notch electronic gear that helps them get even closer to the bad guys.

SF teams can be equipped with different types of remote surveillance sensors, including electromagnetic sensors that can detect artillery, tanks and other vehicles. They work by picking up disruptions to the surrounding magnetic field. They can be placed several hundred yards outside the OP and used to alert the surveillance team to enemy movement. Then you get seismic sensors that pick up vibrations in the earth caused by heavy vehicles moving or artillery rounds landing nearby, but the downside to both these types of sensor is that they aren't always accurate. They will also detect civilian vehicles moving through the same magnetic field, or natural movements in the surrounding earth – meaning false alarms for the patrol. Other equipment is available for hi-tech observation including cameras that can record enemy troop movements and are fitted with night-vision lenses that can be wirelessly and instantly transmitted via SATCOM to high command, acoustic detectors and infrared sensors that can be used to register enemy target's body heat.

Laser range-finders can be also used to pinpoint the distance to the target. These work by firing a light pulse towards the target marker and then measuring the distance by the time it takes for the pulse to 'bounce' off the object and back to the operator. They can also be used by sniper teams to precisely

Electronic gear is all well and good, but the bread and butter of SF surveillance is human intelligence and that's very important, especially in hostile environments where the threat comes from a non-conventional enemy. In a barren, open terrain like Afghanistan, airplanes can't tell the difference between civilian trucks and insurgent ones, and neither can hi-tech sensors. It comes down to the human intelligence of the SF patrol.

measure the distance to the enemy. (In a two-man sniper team one guy will take the data and collate it and the other will operate his weapon.)

This sort of gear can give the head shed an unprecedented picture of the target environment literally as good as being a fly on the wall.

Sometimes the patrol won't have night-vision equipment and they need to rely on their own eyes in the dark. Operators specially train in this technique, because there is a lot more to it than eating carrots. The first thing to do is wait: it takes about half an hour to forty-five minutes for a soldier's eyes to adapt to darkness because the retina's night cells, which function during darkness, are not used in the daytime and it takes a while for the brain to 'switch' between day cells and night cells. (Sometimes operators will wear sunglasses for the day prior, making the transition to night-time vision smoother.)

Once the SF operator is 'acclimatised' to night-time, he must then try and observe a target by scanning it, moving his eyes around the edges of the target. Ideally the operator should train his eye away from the object by a distance equivalent to the width of his fist. 'Off-centre vision' differs from person to person –

some people will find it better to look above, some below, some to the left or right. The operator will have to experiment to find out which works best for him. To identify whether something dark is moving or is just a trick of the brain, the operator should look away from it for about half a minute and look back at it. After doing this a few times, if the target is in the same place, then he can be sure that it's just his mind playing tricks on him. The SF observer must also make sure he gets forty winks now and then. Sleep deprivation can lead to hallucinations during night-time surveillance.

Counter-surveillance equipment is also used by some elite operators, such as the Thermal Imaging Counter Measures (TICM) suit as this decreases the thermal energy that the body produces. Additional cloaking comes in the form of a thermal cover for observation posts. Again this works by masking the thermal energy the body emits and making it harder for the enemy to detect operators. NVGs have a built-in feature called Automatic Brightness Control (ABC) that protects the operator's eyes against sudden flashes of bright light e.g. a white phos grenade exploding.

Locating the enemy by fire, while used by teams carrying out recce tasks and surveillance, is also useful in any contact situation in the field. It's a quick and useful way of sussing out where the guys are coming under fire from, either against themselves or other friendly forces, and how far away the enemy is. Operators will listen out for the distinctive 'thump' (not the 'crack' sound a rifle makes when fired, but the sound that follows it) to understand the direction of the fire. They can then estimate the distance of the enemy by calculating the delay between the 'crack' and the 'thump' – as the 'crack' sound is actually the air being displaced around it, and the 'thump' is the gun being fired, the 'crack' travels faster through the air. By measuring the minute delay between the 'crack' and the 'thump', and bearing in mind that a bullet travels 600m a second a sound at 300m per second, the operator can form a rough guess of the distance of the enemy. When multiple rounds are fired the guys will ignore every shot until the last one and focus on that.

DRAWING SKILLS

In today's hi-tech combat environment, patrols can use mobile comms systems to take real-time photographs of enemy targets and strongholds and instantly and wirelessly send them back to the head shed for evaluation. However, there are situations when the elite operator won't have access to fancy equipment and will have to resort to drawing pictures during the team's recce. For example during a hostage siege in a metropolitan area the first operator to arrive might look to do an emergency recce of the building. This can be very helpful to planning operations, particularly if blueprints for the structure are proving hard to come by.

Drawing is a skill set all by itself, and just like understanding how to fire accurately or freefall from a Hercules, it takes time to learn. First and foremost the drawing has to be accurate, and the soldier has to be able to produce it quickly, because this might be the only view the team has of an enemy position. It doesn't have to rival Monet.

All that's needed is a pen and paper. Ideally the operator should try to make two passes of the target. On the first pass he needs to decide what features he is going to focus on. The details he is looking for are ones that will help plan for the mission, such as:

★ **Doors** – what kind of locks and hinges does the door have? Is it made of wood or metal?

★ **Windows** – are the windows reinforced or darkened? Do they provide the enemy targets with a clear line of sight? Are they ledged or framed (this will affect the team's ability to carry out a rappel insertion)?

★ **Other features** – are there drain pipes the team can use? Is the stronghold a brick or wood structure? What about surrounding trees and shrubbery that might provide concealment for the team during its approach?

With these details tipped in, the operator will then make a second pass, looking to take up a concealed position, perhaps in an area covered by shadow in the corner of an adjacent building, or in a windowed room of a nearby abandoned structure – anywhere that provides him with the best view of the target possible without compromising his position. Here he will complete his sketch, trying to draw the target as the team will see it during their approach, i.e. from the front or to the rear. The operator will also sketch in the surrounding area, including road networks and other infrastructure. Typically representations should stick to different colours for different elements, black for buildings, blue for civilians and friendly forces, and red to show the targets.

Technology is often an incredible force multiplier. During my time in the Regiment, GPS had only really just been made available. GPS units were as big as bricks, and weighed as much. Now they're the size of mobile phones and can fit snugly into an operator's hand. For pinpointing accurate artillery fire, they're invaluable and a big step forward in effective Special Forces operations.

07 ASSAULT

> ONCE THE TEAM HAS DONE A RECCE ON THE TARGET, IT'S TIME TO GET DOWN TO BUSINESS //

Armed to the teeth with a massive variety of firepower, it's down to the patrol to use the intelligence they have gathered to work out the best way of attacking the enemy. There are four different attack options open to a Special Forces unit preparing to launch an assault: Artillery and Air Strikes, Explosives and Attack.

ARTILLERY STRIKES

In order to carry out an effective artillery strike against a target, the team needs to conduct the operation by using an artillery observer, also known as an FAO or Forward Air Operator. The FAO will be situated in an OP, or have sneaked forward from the OP to a vantage point to coordinate the attack. He must have a visual on the target. Using laser rangefinders, target designators or binoculars means that the FAO can be situated as far as 20km away from the target. If he's relying on the naked eye he'll need to be in clear visual radius of the target, aided or unaided. The maximum firing range depends on the nature of the target. Because of the forces required, this is not a type of strike that can be carried out deep behind enemy lines and is difficult to conduct against moving targets, but when the team has the resources and time to prepare for an artillery assault, the results can be deadly.

When in place, the FAO will establish direct contact with the artillery guys. He gives them detailed information about the range and type of the target (e.g. air base, weapons cache, radar installation or terrorist cell HQ), the trajectory needed and the type of shell or fuse needed to neutralise the target, using his GPS system to accurately pinpoint the target location.

Then the fireworks begin. The artillery team opens fire. In the old days, the artillery team would fire an initial smoke round to establish range, but since the introduction of GPS, artillery fire has become much more accurate. Smoke rounds only serve to give the enemy a bit of warning to get their act together and scarper. In the unlikely event that the artillery rounds fall long, short or wide of the target, the fire support specialist gets back on the radio and tells the team to adjust fire, measuring the angle between the last round and the target with something called 'mils'. Mils stands for 'mili-radian' and is a unit of angle measurements, and by calculating roughly the distance in metres between the target and round, then multiplying that by the distance between the FAO and the target, this should give an accurate measurement to within fifty metres of the target – the impact range of a standard artillery round. Once the target range is perfect, the specialist will send the order to 'Fire for effect', which basically means, 'Let them have it'. The specialist will continue to observe the artillery rounds and once he's satisfied the target has been neutralised, he'll radio in to tell the team to end the mission, along with an update on the target's status.

AIR STRIKES

The standard operating procedure for calling in air strikes is pretty much the same as artillery. The FAO will use either a GPS system to verify the target or a laser-target designator (LTD) to 'paint' the target. He will then radio in saying, 'Fast air, fast air'. If he's using GPS, he will give the grid coordinates of the

SAS Blades operating in Iraq during the
2003 war used Harrier jumpjet bombs to
hit key targets and personnel. Using local
intelligence, the operators would close in
on key targets, using surveillance
techniques to get a positive ID on the
target. Once the person's identity had
been established and verified, SAS
spotters would use laser target
designators to mark the target and call
in the artillery strikes. One such
Regiment-led strike helped to neutralise
the notorious Ba'athist 'Chemical Ali'
Hassan al-Majid in Basra in April 2003.
Although al-Majid survived the Harrier
bombing he was subsequently arrested
and put on trial.

target; an LTD system will automatically do that for him. The FAO will then be given a Time on Target – the time at which the missile will hit the target. This is important because, if the FAO has had to sneak up close to the target to verify or paint it, he'll need to know how much time he has to withdraw to a safe distance. Depending on the combat situation in the air, he might only have a few minutes – or it could be as long as several hours.

Air strikes are good when the SF patrol is deep behind enemy lines and lacks artillery support for smashing a target to pieces. But the downside is that air strikes have a higher chance of something going wrong. I'm not basing this on statistics, just from personal experience. But every time I've heard of a strike go wrong, it's been from the air, not from artillery. There were several incidents of blue-on-blue in the first Gulf War, and in the more recent Iraq campaign, quite a few documented cases where armoured personnel carriers were hit by friendly forces aircraft.

EXPLOSIVES

Special Forces engineers have an important role to play in today's conflicts, literally building bridges and repairing civilian infrastructure to win hearts and minds. In environments as hostile and tetchy as Iraq and Afghanistan, that's critical. But for my money, their primary goal is still to blow stuff up!

Demolitions are useful when the team isn't able to call on air or artillery support to eliminate a target, especially in situations when there is no clear air superiority or where, for political reasons, it's not been possible to move a large ground force including artillery units into a country. So it's down to the boys on the ground to destroy a key enemy installation.

Explosives can also be used to penetrate a secure structure or territory, eliminating obstacles that stand in the way of the SF team and success. When I was working with BOPE in the favelas, a common trick of the local drug gangs was to secure makeshift bollards made from oil drums filled with cement, to the middle of the roads, making it impossible for the BOPE 'Skull' vehicles to drive down. The only solution was to blow them up so the team could continue its patrol.

Explosives are a serious business and you can't afford to fool around with them. When an explosive device detonates it violently changes into highly compressed gas, creating a shockwave that obliterates everything in its path. The type, density, quantity and placing of the explosive affects how big this shockwave is, and how much destruction and devastation it causes to the surrounding area. For that reason explosive charges are carried separately from detonators.

When a larger explosion is required the operator makes a hole in the main explosive charge and fills it with primer, a highly volatile explosive substance. The blasting cap sets off the primer which in turn sets off the main explosive. This chain reaction is incredibly powerful so if the team is nearby and looking, for example, to blow a hole in a wall, they will sandbag the exposed side of the explosive to direct the shockwave into the wall and shield themselves from the blast.

The team will also need to take into account the type of target they must take out. For buildings made primarily out of concrete, a cover charge of a highly combustible substance such as gasoline or wheat flour, when used in conjunction with a regular charge, will incinerate the building – the flour or gasoline ignites in the compressed gas atmosphere of the charge, creating a fireball that no one is surviving, simple as that. Steel structured buildings are a lot harder to demolish. The team will need to use special steel-cutting charges such as plastic explosives like C4 or sheet charges like MI 18. These are great for ripping through steel chains, cables and sheets. The rule is that width is better than thickness, and for best results, the charge should run the whole length of the intended explosive area.

The placement of explosives is also important when sabotaging aircraft lying on an enemy runway or guarded in a hangar, or tanks or missile launchers. A single charge may destroy part of the target, but carefully placed smaller charges at each of the target's critical points (its engine, weapons and fuel tanks) will put it out of commission for good. The same principle applies when faced with taking out bridges or demolishing railway lines. There's also a basic reason for targeting weak points rather than seeking to cause mass destruction and mayhem – carrying enough explosives would be impossible for the demolitions guy, so it's very much out of necessity too.

When blowing up bridges there are three basic collapse mechanisms – see-saw collapse (placing two or more explosive charges on a multispan bridge), beam collapse (used for single span bridges by placing the charge in the middle of the bridge structure) and member without support collapse (two explosive charges on a single stretch of a multispan structure,

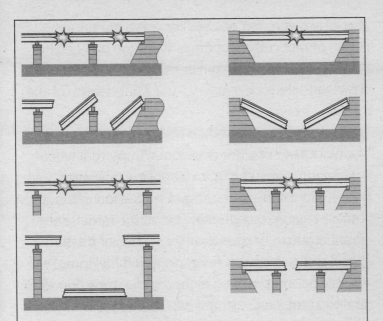

Single span and multi-span bridges can be demolished in a variety of ways. Top left – see-saw collapse, where two beams are separately targeted; bottom left – member without support collapse where two separately placed charges drop a section off a single-span bridge; top right – beam collapse, used on a single span bridge with a weak structure; and bottom right – cantilever effect for single charges placed on a multi-span bridge.

causing the section between the two charges to collapse). The demolitions guy is always looking for the weakest link and to use the minimum amount of explosive material, whether it's the cables on a suspension bridge or the girders on a truss bridge.

Explosives can also be used for creating helicopter LZs, using timber-cutting charges to flatten a gentle sloping area of mountain or hillside so the helicopter can land safely.

Demolitions experts should also be able to manufacture tripwires and booby traps, which slow the enemy down during exfiltration. US SF teams are given a range of camouflaged percussion detonators that are simple to operate. The M1A2 is one of the detonators that American elite professionals use – it has a cap protector, a firing pin assembly and a handle pull ring with an eight-second delay. Removing the cap protector, the operator screws the M1A2 detonator into the explosive material, removes the small cotter pin, and then pulls the ring to fire. Using field materials this can be converted into a tripwire that releases the ring when the wire is breached.

In addition, demolitions experts in an SF patrol should have the ability to conjure up improvised and home-made explosives. For example, pipe hand grenades can be constructed by placing a blast cap with a fuse cord attached into one end of a sealed iron pipe and filling it with explosives. Wine bottle charges are made by placing explosives into a wine bottle that has had the top half removed, packing it in and then placing a

Nowadays the lads fighting in Iraq and Afghanistan are dealing with a lot of Improvised Explosive Devices (IEDs) set by the enemy to try and inflict greater casualties. IEDs have been in use since Vietnam, and were used by the IRA in Northern Ireland, but have become the weapon of choice in Iraq, where insurgents have used the latest technology to create a vast array of IEDs. These are a lot more difficult to detect than standard roadside bombs. IEDs can be sewn into the bellies of dead animals or placed inside the chassis of old cars. The explosives can be detonated by passive infrared sensors wired up to the road. When the first vehicle in a patrol breaks the sensor, the detonator is pressed and the bomb explodes on the third vehicle. IEDs can also be activated by using a mobile phone – and the results are often devastating and bloody. It's just another example of how operators must never underestimate the enemy's capabilities, and keep their eyes and ears sharp at all times.

blasting cap on top. Wine bottle charges can penetrate several inches of armour and are excellent for disabling a tank or vehicle, by placing it on or next to the engine. Home-made explosives, from domestic materials such as ammonium nitrate compounds and home-made black powder, can be useful in emergency situations, although they are more volatile.

ATTACK

Sometimes the situation calls for a straightforward attack rather than the use of remote artillery or C4 – and this is where attack action drills in. There are two types of action drill – Immediate (also known as Emergency Response) and Deliberate Action. Which one is used depends on the circumstances facing the SF team.

DELIBERATE ACTION // In the field or behind enemy lines, deliberate action techniques can be employed as the target is unlikely to be expecting immediate attack, and the assault team can plan strategically for the attack. Long-range surveillance and use of OPs will allow the team to build up a picture of the target, assessing its defence strengths and weaknesses and the type of weapons or attack best suited to the target.

**A Deliberate Action is
initiated following a
thorough and detailed plan
of attack, based on the view
of those in command of the
situation that taking no
action will result in loss of
civilian life.**

If the SF team's mission is to attack an enemy terrorist stronghold, for example, the team will observe enemy activity around the fortress, building up a detailed survey of enemy troop routines and movement. The team will rely on its ability to get into perfect firing positions, where they can lay down rounds on the maximum number of targets from the most concealed position. In Afghanistan, when SF lads had to carry out an assault against a mud fort overrun by captured al-Qaeda fighters, they took up positions on the fort walls, turning the ground inside the fortress into a kill zone.

Deliberate actions can be noisy or silent. In a noisy deliberate action assault, the sniper team will take up positions around the stronghold. Dressed in camouflage such as the Ghillie suits (which resemble heavy foliage) used by the Special Task Force guys in Sri Lanka, the snipers will establish a clear line of sight with the targets.

In any assault however there are several key phases that form an order of battle. In the preparation for an attack, the team will establish a **Forming Up Point (FUP)** in an assembly area close to the target area. Communicating in hand signals and whispers the operators will rehearse the attack plan, check equipment and, moving slowly, get into pre-established positions for the main assault. Then begins the **Approach Phase** with the operators heading for the target, moving narrowly at first then fanning out as they approach the target area, putting rounds down and performing fire manoeuvres. When they are within 40 or 50m of the enemy position they enter the **break-in** phase – the guys will now be in position to breach the enemy defensive positions. Once this has been achieved, the team will transition into the **Fight Through** phase, where the operators will maintain their attacking momentum, carrying out a coordinated attack against disparate elements of the enemy forces. The key is to maximise the confusion and fear caused by the operators' assault, consolidating their position and exploiting this by pursuing any fleeing enemy forces or encircling them to prevent a corridor of escape and then letting them have it.

There are several forms of attack manoeuvre employed by operators. **Frontal attacks** are, as the name suggests, designed to attack the enemy at the forward position and should be avoided at all costs – the front is likely to be the most reinforced and focused part of the stronghold as it is where the enemy will be expecting the attack to occur. **Breaching manoeuvres** are used to smash through a single defensive point in the enemy position and focus the assault effort – good when intel indicates a weak point in the enemy lines. **Flanking attacks** to the left, right and rear of the stronghold focus the assault on the areas of the enemy position least likely to feature adequate defences because they won't be expecting to get hit here. **Infiltrating attacks** are conducted by manoeuvring around the enemy position undetected, as a precursor to launching an attack from a highly advantageous position and detailed recce intel.

If the team is preparing a night attack they will look to keep the plan stupid-simple as any complicated battle plans will be doubly difficult to carry out effectively at night. The guys will rehearse a night op over and over and use tracer rounds during the main assault to illuminate the enemy.

The sniper team will have been recceing out the area, identifying the best angle of attack, making notes on obstacles and the relative strength and weakness of enemy positions, as well as enemy routines and patrols. They will be keeping an eye out for any weak points in the target that would make an ideal position to launch the assault.

Leading the attack will be the forward element. They are charged with spearheading the attack on the position or installation and laying down fire. Their first job is to plant Claymore mines as close to the ambush area – also known as the Kill Zone – as possible. Claymores are effective up to 110 yards, but are at their most lethal at half that distance, so that is how close the operators will want to get. Once set, they will detonate the Claymores simultaneously using clackers. It's vital to start putting rounds in as soon as the Claymores have detonated, when the enemy is at its most confused and disoriented.

To the left and right of the forward element are the fire support group who will be laying down sustained fire on the enemy during the attack using heavy machine guns like the GPMG (General Purpose Machine Gun), a 7.62×61 mm belt-fed weapon that can be mounted on a tripod or on the WMIK Land Rover or even on the side of a helicopter. With a two-man crew operating it, the Gimpy is capable of laying down 750 rounds per minute, at a distance of up to 1800 metres, trapping the enemy in a brutal killing zone. The fire support group may also utilise sniper weapons for precision fire as well as harassing fire, in a tactic also known as 'Fix and Strike'.

Fix and Strike is the art of locking the enemy into a fixed position using sustained fire. By fixing the enemy he is unable to move and secure his position, return fire accurately, or escape. In a Deliberate Action, fix and strike tactics are employed once the initial assault has begun, and is usually conducted using heavy machine guns like the Gimpy and LAWs as well.

The key to a successful fire support action is mobility. They will not be operating from a single fixed position, instead the guys will put rounds down, neutralising and pinning the enemy targets into vulnerable positions, and move on before the enemy can train defensive fire onto them. As a non-static force they can take out a variety of targets at both the frontal and deeper enemy lines.

To the rear, a security team keeps guard and protects the escape route, keeping a look-out for any additional and unaccounted enemy forces that might try and launch a counter-attack.

The snipers begin the attack, taking out visual targets that pose the most immediate threat to the forward assault squad. The forward element is then charged with neutralising the main enemy threat. If the mission objective includes taking a prisoner, obtaining important documents or technology or rescuing a POW, a 'snatch' team will be designated to retrieve the objective while the rest of the attack element provides covering fire. In some deliberate actions in the field, it's necessary to combine this front assault with an air or artillery strike in order to neutralise enemy combatants or destroy any possible escape route for the enemy such as rail or aircraft transport. But combining the two carries an additional risk – in one assault on an Afghan mud fort, an air strike missed its target, incinerating a bunch of Northern Alliance guys. In the chaos of battle, things don't always go to plan.

Once the ambush is complete, the enemy soldiers defeated, prisoners rounded up, communications out of order and all mission objectives complete, the team will then fall back to the escape route. If they are making an exit on foot they will look to plant delayed-detonation Claymores behind them to hold up the enemy and allow the team to slip away towards the exfiltration route, where the waiting helicopter will pick them up and take them back to HQ for a warm brew and decent scoff.

In some cases it's better for the SF team to take a silent approach. This involves the snipers picking off targets at long range, while the forward assault team sneaks up to the base covertly, taking out enemy combatants with silenced weapons. The idea here is that the objective can be neutralised without setting off a major alarm. This is useful if the team is concerned that an open firefight could attract unwanted attention, either from nearby ground forces or if there is information to suggest that a noisy attack could trigger further loss of innocent lives.

The Claymore will blanket a 60° area in front of it in overlapping arcs of steel ball shrapnel.

Once contact is inevitable, the SF team reacts swiftly.

Establishing a baseline with Sri Lankan STF operators.

Skis are a great way of moving rapidly across exposed land.

Regiment lads in Mountain Troop practising mountain warfare climbing techniques.

Getting ready to move in on an exercise with Israel's Magav border police, tooled up with a 203 grenade launcher mounted underneath the Colt Commando. The guy on the right has a side-mounted head cam – when he neutralizes a target he will look down to record the face and confirm the kill. They tried to fit out the lads in the Regiment with head-cams but mysteriously they kept breaking down, accidentally knocking against walls!

Blowing up a cocaine plant in Colombia using C4 and det cord to create multiple explosives that go off at the same time for maximum effectiveness. The cartels won't be using this plantation again anytime soon.

IEDs are a real problem for operators – they can be disguised as almost anything and cause serious damage, as this jeep belonging to the Sri Lankan STF demonstrates.

Elite operators will see action in a variety of combat theatres, from the dusty, confined streets of Iraq through to boat-based recces down rivers and waterways.

Israeli Magav operators practising target neutralization. The guy with the shotgun has it loaded with a breaching round, either a Hatton round made of powered lead wax, or a bean-bag, to blast open the window. The team then verify the target and once they have a positive ID, they let him have it, spraying the car with rounds. The exit rounds at the other side of the vehicle are much larger than the entry rounds — imagine the kind of damage these rounds do when they enter the human body.

Explosive entry into the Killing House with Sri Lanka's Special Task Force guys. After blowing the brick wall open the team enters. My weapon suffered a stoppage and the guys behind me had to cover my back. Teams have to prepare for unexpected situations, because things can and do go wrong on operations.

US Navy SEALS preparing for an insertion. The SEALS are one of the world's elite fighting units.

Finding a good firing position is critical to a successful assault. Operators will take into account several factors when considering a firing position – freedom of access to his weapons systems, cover from small-arms fire and grenade and mortar attacks, and a position that provides them with the widest possible view of the target area so they can lay down a wide arc of direct fire.

FIGHT TO WIN

Ambushes are an effective way of using a small force to inflict serious damage on a much larger one. When an elite patrol is inserted into enemy territory, hitting them at resupply points or along communications lines can destabilise a sizeable armed force.

In urban environment counter-terrorism, deliberate actions can often occur in hostage-rescue scenarios. In a situation where the terrorists (X-rays) have started executing hostages (Yankees), the team needs to intervene to prevent the further loss of life.

During the Iranian Embassy siege of 1980, negotiations continued and military action was put on ice as long as the hostages were alive. In a delicate situation, an assault can escalate violence and put innocent lives in danger. But when the terrorists killed press attaché Abbas Lavasani and threw his body outside, the decision was taken that an assault was the necessary course of action to prevent more hostages' lives being endangered.

Let's say that X-rays have taken control of a building in a downtown metropolitan area and have begun executing hostages. The time for negotiation is over, and violence is now the only solution. The elite team, either a Special Forces unit trained in counter-

Military action means dialogue has broken down and the situation can only be changed through the use of force. It should always be the last resort; never the first.

terrorism techniques like the SAS or SBS, or an elite paramilitary unit like BOA, must now take charge of the situation from the local police authorities.

Deliberate action information will have been collected during the early stages of the siege when negotiators will have been liaising with the X-rays to give up the hostages and surrender themselves. From a command and control centre close by, the mission commander will assemble all the information he receives regarding the location, X-rays and hostages. If this is on home territory, blueprints of the building will give him a detailed understanding of the layout, possible escape routes, traps and so on. The commander will be constantly in communication with the rest of the team, both before and during the assault. He will mainly be relying on his elite snipers.

Snipers will have positioned themselves on surrounding buildings to get a visual line of sight on the windows of the target building. Their sniper rifles will have been fitted with devices that are wired back to the command and control centre. Each time the sniper spots an X-ray he presses the button. Back in the ops room a light flashes on and off when the button is pressed. The commander is looking at these lights switching on and off to give him an

Snipers aren't just there to cut down the X-rays. They are primarily there during the planning stage for the passage of information to the command and control centre. They're the eyes and ears of the operation, and must practise the art of *viewing without being seen* – hiding in the shadows, wearing camouflage.

understanding of X-ray numbers. If there are seven snipers positioned around the stronghold and seven lights all come on at once, he knows he is dealing with seven different X-rays. The snipers will also be using advanced listening devices to help build up an incredibly detailed picture about X-ray numbers and movement that helps the commander to plan for the attack.

At the same time an assault squad will be preparing for their part of the attack, the frontal assault. They'll be decked out in an all-black one-piece suit made of flame-retardant fibres in order to make them less visible targets to X-rays when entering the building, as well as fireproof elbow and knee pads to protect them against broken glass when making a crash window entrance.

When the green light is given, the commander will tell everybody to get in position. Now everyone radios in to confirm they're in position and they wait for the commander's signal. He's looking for the snipers to flash as many lights on the box as possible. Once he has six or seven lights, he will then say in a slow, controlled voice, 'Stand by, stand by, go.' When he says that second 'stand by' you know there's no going back now. It's on.

Deliberate Action plans will always change as more information is passed on and revealed.

The snipers fire simultaneously at their targets. Hopefully the snipers will take out all the X-rays in one swift blow. As they open fire the assault team moves in through the main doors, mopping up as they go along. The snipers will have to be on high alert, because an explosive entry by the assault team could fuse the lights, plunging the building into darkness and increasing the chance of a blue-on-blue (friendly fire casualty).

IMMEDIATE ACTION / EMERGENCY RESPONSE //

This is when the team has no time to plan an attack in detail, and has to launch the assault straight away. A good example would be the recent terrorist attacks in Mumbai. Clearly those guys weren't interested in negotiations – they just wanted to kill as many Yankees as possible to fulfil their own twisted fantasy.

In the case of an Immediate Action the command and control centre would have access to nowhere near the same level of information as a Deliberate Action. There probably won't have been the time to position snipers around the target, let alone the time for them to gather detailed knowledge of X-ray movements. The commanding officer will mostly refer

Immediate Action / Emergency Response plans should only be implemented when the situation is absolutely critical. They're less likely to succeed. With intelligence limited, the plan must be uncomplicated – or, as we used to say in the Regiment, keep it stupid-simple.

In an Immediate Action drill the team are looking to maximise the mission's chances of success by using speed, aggression, teamwork, fast accurate shooting and, most of all, the element of surprise. By playing to their strengths, they stand the best chance of suppressing the enemy and rescuing civilians. In the SAS we practised Immediate Action drills using the Killing House training set-up, something I was able to get stuck into again during my time alongside BOA, Poland's elite police force. The Killing House is specially built for CQB training and allows operators to use live rounds, something they wouldn't normally get to do in a training scenario. But live rounds tense you up, reminding you that this is real. The walls of the Killing House are rubber-coated so that rounds don't pass through them or ricochet off them and injure an operator. The partitions separating each room can be adjusted, changing the layout of the Killing House so the challenge facing the guys is different each time.

to a chalkboard that has red and blue markers on it — red for X-rays and blue for Yankees.

INSERTION OF TEAM // Depending on the type of building the team are assaulting, they will enter either by windows, skylights, walls or roof. Entering from the roof access point requires the team rappelling or fast-roping onto the roof by helicopter and then locating the roof access stairwell. They will need to have an entry tool in case the stairwell is locked. Windows and skylights can be accessed by ladder or fast rope and placing an explosive charge on the window. Walls can be penetrated using devices such as the Harvey Wall Banger, a water-filled, plastic projectile wall-breaching cannon that fires at a high velocity, and it is much less likely to injure Yankees than traditional explosive entries.

ROOM ENTRY // Elite operators will use a three-man room entry formation. Number 1 takes position on the hinge side of the door, giving him maximum visibility when the door is breached. Number 2 takes up his position behind Number 1, ready to follow him into the room. Most doors swing inward, but for outward doors, these positions are reversed.

On the commander's signal, Number 3 blows the hinges off the door with a shotgun loaded with

'Hatton' rounds (breaching rounds made of metal powder in a wax that can be used to blow off hinges at close range without the risk of ricocheting shrapnel associated with standard buckshot). Number 2 will then throw a 'distraction' such as a flash bang, into the room. Now Number 1 enters fast. He's looking for the maximum centre of activity in the room and quickly assesses and suppresses the primary threat, aiming for the torso first in order to cause maximum damage (the torso contains a lot of the vital organs such as the heart and lungs), finishing with a head shot to make sure the X-ray has gone over to the dark side.

Beforehand the team will have rehearsed which way each man is going – if Number 1 enters the room and goes to the left, Number 2 goes to the right. This way the team clears the room efficiently and rapidly. Behind them Number 3 drops the entry tool and reverts to his weapon ready at the door, offering covering support and keeping a close eye on the area outside the door in case of an attack by unaccounted X-rays located elsewhere in the building.

MULTI-ROOM ASSAULT // More often than not, when faced with an Immediate Action scenario, the team will have to clear more than one room, and maybe even more than one level of a building. In

Room assault. Two operators are positioned on the hinge side of the door, with the third operator, armed with the breaching device, opposite them.

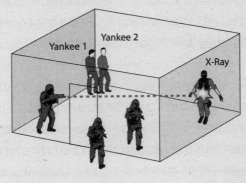

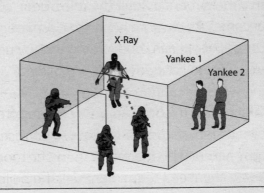

these situations, the teams will have to clear each room of a floor or multiple floors in sequence, operating in 3- or 4-man teams, and having no more than 4 rooms to clear each (the time it takes to reach and clear 5 rooms or more is considered too long for a rapid assault mission to be successful).

The 3-man team will use the same technique to enter each room as a single-room assault. Upon entering the room, the shout 'Clear room', is given by Number 1. As he's the first guy to enter the room he is prepared for contact. Number 1 then engages any X-rays. After he's dealt with the maximum threat Number 2 enters and makes sure the room is secure and the threats have been neutralised. He then gives the shout 'Room clear', throws a glow stick in to mark it out and the team moves on to the next room.

In a multi-room assault the role of the Number 3 guy becomes much more important. As well as providing cover and opening doors using entry tools, he must also take on the added responsibility of assault. In a multi-room situation Number 1 and Number 2 guys might enter a room, suppress an X-ray and find that a connecting room door is open, so while Number 1 is busy neutralising the threat in the first room, Number 2 and Number 3 team members must proceed immediately on to the connecting room and engage any X-rays.

MULTI-FLOOR ASSAULT //
In this scenario the team will execute the same principle as the multi-room assault, but using several teams entering the building from different insertion points to guarantee maximum effectiveness. One team will go in through the front of the building, or by using a controlled explosion against a brick wall on one side of the structure. A second team will then fast-rope onto the roof and make its way down the stairwell. At the same time, a third team will prepare to crash the windows by rappelling down the side of the building, or using ladders from the ground if they know the windows can be opened from the outside. The operators will use every window. If there are five windows on that floor, the team will have five guys rappelling in. They will need a high level of marksmanship and fitness to be able to hit a moving target, one-handed, swinging from the end of a rope.

The attack has to be simultaneous from all groups of the assault team. As soon as all the guys are in the building, to avoid any possible blue-on-blues, the commander based at the command and control centre will be focusing hard on his chalkboard, moving

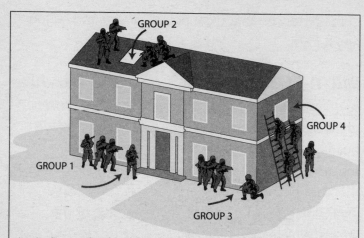

GROUP 2

GROUP 4

GROUP 1

GROUP 3

Multi-floor assaults require at least four teams – one to gatecrash through the front, one to enter via the roof, a third to crash the windows and a fourth to enter via a side door, window or detonate and breach a wall.

red and blue markers around and maintaining constant contact with the SF squad. There's no messing around here. Comms are clear and simple so that the commander's picture of the assault is as accurate as possible. The area of each team's attack is spelled out loud and clear. He's vital to the success of the attack as it will be his ability to form as up-to-the-minute a picture of the attack as possible and coordinate the assault effectively with the team. Believe me, the combat commander really earns his money in immediate actions – they're the fastest games of chess he'll ever play.

An immediate action is the worst option in any assault – you're going in half-cocked and possibly into a situation where you will be exposed to a lot of danger. As you're blind, a lot hinges on your reactions and training – and the skills of the mission commander.

Once every room has been cleared and all Yankees and X-rays are plasticuffed the commander will give the signal, 'Evacuate building' and the team will proceed down the stairwell to the reception. The reception party checks every Yankee to make sure no X-rays have disguised themselves as hostages. It's vital for the team to properly check and clear each hostage. Stockholm Syndrome can mean that hostages might form close bonds with their captors, protecting or hiding terrorists from the team and allowing them to escape. Only by conducting a thorough search can this type of situation be avoided.

There are two other attacks that SF teams must be capable of carrying out: tubular assaults and front contact.

TUBULAR ASSAULTS // These cover any type of attack that takes place in a confined vehicle environment – trains, planes and buses.

Let's imagine that the hostage siege situation I've talked about takes a different course, and the terrorists reach a deal with the police negotiators: they want an aircraft to fly them to safety in a neutral country. Once they are in safe territory they will release the hostages. The negotiators agree in principle to this, and tell the X-rays they will prepare a bus to transport them to the airport.

The key to tubular actions is that you place it where you want it. In situations like this, the team has the ability to set up the time and place of the assault – if they play their cards right.

When the X-rays emerge with the Yankees, if they're not completely stupid they will have placed black hoods over everyone in the party, making it hard for surveillance officers to establish how many terrorists there are. The X-rays might even cover the windows of the bus with black bin liners. As the bus makes its way towards the airport, the SF team will create an 'end route' where they will block off the bus. Waiting to pounce will be the SF unit. On the flank or rear of the bus snipers will be covertly set up – but it's really important that the area is clear of the general public in case it gets messy.

Once the bus has been blocked off, the team springs into action. Two teams are used to carry out a tubular attack: a **containment team** will already be in place, with window covermen ready to mount ladders against the sides of the bus, arrest/evacuation team members to suppress the terrorists and anyone who

Choosing a good end route is essential. No self-respecting terrorist is going to allow the bus to go down dead-end roads. If they suspect that they're being led away from their chosen destination, they could start executing hostages in retaliation. It's best to try and block the transport at a bend.

tries to escape from the bus (they will also have attack dogs with them to pounce on any fleeing X-rays), and special breaching equipment to bust open the main doors of the bus. There may also be snipers placed in positions around the bus to provide cover for the team.

The **entry team** will launch the assault into the bus. Debussing from a helicopter or an urban assault vehicle, the entry team lines up to the rear of the target with one or two team members posted at the driver's door. This is important because, if the driver is an X-ray, he will have an unrestricted view of the

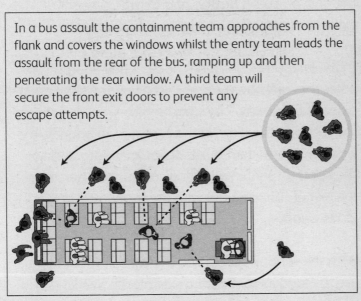

In a bus assault the containment team approaches from the flank and covers the windows whilst the entry team leads the assault from the rear of the bus, ramping up and then penetrating the rear window. A third team will secure the front exit doors to prevent any escape attempts.

interior and exterior of the bus thanks to his side and rear mirrors – giving him early warning of an attack.

The containment team will position ladders against the windows of the bus. If the bus is non-mobile (i.e. a terrorist has taken control of a bus and is not expecting a siege) then the team will look to use a distraction – such as the sound of passing trains or cars – to mask the sound of the ladders hitting the side of the bus. The containment team will use detonator poles to breach the windows. A detonator pole is a pole that has an explosive element at the tip. When it is up against the window the guy holding the pole presses a button and a small amount of explosive goes off, blowing open the window.

In the event that the team doesn't have detonator poles they will have to breach the windows the good old-fashioned way – by smashing them with a sharp tool. Striking the glass in the centre is no good as the windows on modern buses are often reinforced, so the operator should aim for a corner and then rake the rest of the glass out with the tool or the butt of his weapon.

With the windows breached the containment team use the ladders to mount a side attack. Working in

Tubular assaults on targets such as buses are tricky because the view facing out of the vehicle is better than the vlew facing into it, giving X-rays a distinct advantage. That, as well as the fact that a bus can hold between 40-60 people in a confined space, tests an operator's skills to the limit. Planning, handgun ability, coordination and speed is vital.

pairs, one guy holds the ladder in place whilst the other ascends, facing into the bus via the window gap and firing upon X-ray targets. In Mexico, working with the *Policia Federal* I saw a variation of this when one partner wrapped his arms around the other guy's legs and lifted him up to the window.

At the same time, the entry team mounts its assault from the rear, breaking the rear window in the same way before entering on poles and moving up the bus. They will move up the bus, clearing it aisle by aisle and suppressing X-rays. If everyone on the bus is wearing hoods the SF team will target those holding weapons. Nobody is allowed to move off the bus until the team has cleared every aisle and accounted for all passengers. Once everyone has been plasticuffed they are led off the bus and laid out in front of it.

For **aircraft assault**, a clear and simple plan is best — again, keep it stupid-simple. I can't emphasise enough how important that mantra is. More complicated plans are more likely to fail. The guys will need to have a complete understanding of the various entry and escape hatches and doors on the aircraft, in order to plan for a multiple entry assault. If there is time, the team will find a smaller model of the aircraft, or a similar one, and practise the execution of the plan. However, even the exact same model of aircraft may not be identical in layout and features, as planes tend to be modified for specific routes and airline requirements.

Aircraft assaults require a larger group of operators than other types of vehicular siege. Depending on the type of plane, there could be upwards of 200 hysterical hostages to deal with – a nightmare for any unit. Getting the hostages out rapidly is also essential as the chances of the terrorists hiding from the team are much greater when they are surrounded by Yankees.

In most cases, due to the nose shape of the aircraft, the team will approach from the tail. This used to be the natural blindspot on an aircraft but some planes now come fitted with CCTV cameras on the tail which the flight crew can access. This again shows the importance of having a detailed understanding of the plane prior to mounting the assault.

Entry to an aircraft can be made through the main doors, emergency doors, escape roof hatches, maintenance hatches and sometimes the baggage hatches, although these aren't always linked to the main interior of the aircraft. A minimum of two entry points will be used for the assault. The more the

Germany's elite counter-terrorism unit, GSG 9 (*Grenzschutzgruppe 9*) is considered to be one of the most effective units of its kind in operation around the world. Their assault on Lufthansa Flight 181 is a prime example of how to carry out an aircraft assault. The flight had been hijacked by Palestinian terrorists mid-flight and diverted to the Somali capital of Mogadishu where they issued an ultimatum that they would destroy the plane and kill all the hostages unless Red Army Faction prisoners were released. Refusing to negotiate, the German government ordered GSG 9 to intervene. The operators carried out detailed rehearsals on a Boeing 737 jet.

Launching the assault, the thirty operators split into six groups of five and approached the plane from its blind spot at the rear. They were able to enter the aircraft through escape hatches located under the fuselage and above the wings of the plane, climbing up using aluminium ladders.

The operation lasted less than ten minutes, with all the terrorists suppressed and at no loss of life to the hostages on board. As aircraft assaults go, it's a textbook example of how to do it.

In any tubular assault, detailed knowledge of the vehicle is vital – make of vehicle, access points, emergency locking systems, engine location, lighting and visibility: all of these factors can help an SF team to make the mission a success.

better. Remember, in aircraft assaults the objective is to clear the maximum area of the plane in the shortest possible time. Using multiple entry points also means that if one entry point proves unsuccessful, the assault can still continue.

The main danger to operators with an aircraft assault doesn't come from the terrorists, but from each other. Multiple entries in a confined space in an unfamiliar environment raises the chances of a blue-on-blue, so the team has to be sure when they engage. Of course, they also have to watch out for onboard civilians. They're likely to be scared witless and controlling them, reducing panic and maintaining order is key to the success of the mission.

FRONT CONTACT // Front contacts are initiated by scout patrols operating ahead of a main task force. Their job is to scout out the area ahead of the main force and suppress any patrols that might be waiting to ambush the task force. In environments where a team is fighting against a mobile, skilled guerrilla army in terrain ideally suited to an ambush like jungle or swamp, front contacts are essential to prevent costly ambushes that sap morale as well as troop strength. Front contacts are different to a deliberate action as the team isn't planning an assault on an

When carrying out a front contact it's important to use speed and aggression to hit the enemy as hard as possible and then extract as quickly as you can. That way, the maximum damage can be inflicted on the enemy whilst sustaining the minimum casualties for the SF patrol.

enemy position – just prepared to deal with a threat if it emerges. You need to remember that your first line of defence is your wits. Your second is your weapon. Make sure you engage your brain before the trigger.

In the jungles in Sri Lanka when I was working with the Special Task Force, front contacts are part of everyday life in their fight against the Tamil Tigers – and I got to see it up close for myself in intense training drills. Travelling in two-man teams on modified Yamaha 225 scrambler motorbikes (the guy on the back carries a weapon and can lay down fire while the other guy drives) helps the patrol negotiate small roads that a car would struggle on, as well as avoiding landmines in a country that is absolutely riddled with them after more than thirty years of internal conflict. When the patrol makes contact with the enemy the guys on the back start firing and then execute a running dismount to form a line of defence.

The bikes now turn around and point towards the escape corridor whilst the other guys take out the enemy soldiers. Once the enemy has been suppressed the guys release smoke charges to mask their retreat and run back to their motorbikes. As they mount, the bikes tear off down the road and through the escape corridor, back towards the main task force.

08 GETTING OUT

> SPEAKING FROM PERSONAL EXPERIENCE, I KNOW THAT NOT ALL SPECIAL OPS GO EXACTLY ACCORDING TO PLAN //

One of my mottoes is that things can always get worse – and it pays to plan bearing that in mind. When a patrol team is compromised, they go into Escape and Evasion (E&E) mode. This system plans for their safe emergency extraction from a lethally hostile environment.

At the planning phase, operators will be given instructions on the E&E procedure for the mission, Including the establishment of an evacuation corridor and the setting up of emergency extraction points where, for the duration of the mission, helicopters will land at pre-assigned times each day in case the patrol gets split up and loses radio contact. They will also rehearse cover stories to tell their captors in the event that they are ambushed and imprisoned – it's important that all members of the patrol tell exactly the same story. If the interrogator picks up inconsistencies between their stories, he knows someone is lying.

E&E procedures are the most important part of any plan.

In a situation when an operator is captured, his best chance of escaping from the enemy is in those vital first few minutes. At this point, confusion is at its maximum, the enemy forces are still recovering from the firefight and reorganising and the operator must try and make a break for it if he can. The rule is that the longer the operator is in captivity, the lower his chances of escaping are, because he will get passed deeper down the enemy chain, and the deeper he goes, the tighter the security ring becomes.

There are some Standard Operating Procedures (SOPs) that all elite operators must follow when taking part in an E&E manoeuvre:

★ **Only move at night** – to minimise the chances of detection, moving when human activity is at its lowest is best.

★ **Stay well clear of human habitation** – even straying too close to animal enclosures on farms is liable to compromise the soldier's cover.

Choosing a secluded hide is the best way of avoiding detection. In the Regiment I once stood for twelve hours in a swamp filled with filthy sewage in Belize. I didn't choose the location for its luxuries, obviously. I chose it because I knew the hunting force would not pay very close attention to such a foul environment, and that would increase my chances of survival.

★ **Establish a suitable Lying-Up Point (LUP)** –
before resting for the night it's vital that the soldier
selects somewhere he is less likely to be discovered
by tracking teams, sniffer dogs and other hunter
forces. For example, the north side of a slope will
be under shadow because of the direction of the
sun. I've hidden in the desert in cow feeders or
buried under leaves in ditches. Finding the dirtiest,
wettest, smelliest hide to rest up in is best. Dogs
are less likely to be sent into low vegetation for fear
of damaging their eyes. It's important not to stay
in the same LUP for more than twenty-four hours.

★ **Keep water topped up** – the one thing an
operator on the run cannot do without is water.
Dehydration is different from thirst. If you're
dehydrated you will have a weak pulse, your hands
and feet will be cold and your lips will turn blue. In
addition your mental faculties will be affected. Your
mind will feel foggy and confused and it will be
hard to complete even the most basic of tasks. At
any chance he should be looking to top up his two
water bottles, and make calculated decisions on
the spot about the cleanliness of a certain water
supply. For example, if you walk 2 or 3 metres
up a fast-flowing river and there's nothing dead
in there, it's probably safe to drink. Water

flows downhill, so if you are near to a valley or depression chances are you'll be able to locate a stream. If there is no apparent surface water and the landscape looks barren then you can look for vegetation nearby and dig a shallow well. In arctic environments, transforming snow into drinkable water is time-consuming. Better to locate a nearby ice source, such as a frozen river, and melt it in a container.

★ **Don't get careless** – for example, if you're hungry and haven't eaten for a number of days, the hunger can become overwhelming and force you to do things that could compromise your chances of survival. If you're famished and manage to snare an animal, you have to remember to clean out the intestines before eating them, or check for discolouration and spots on the kidneys. In the arctic, eating a polar bear's liver is potentially fatal as it contains a very high dosage of vitamin A. If you turn very sick because of carelessness, your chances of survival will go down the pan. Similarly, it's important to be disciplined when it comes to personal hygiene. Keeping your hands, hair and teeth clean is important. Operators can make soap from animal fat and wood ashes by cooking the fat and pouring the grease into a container, collecting

water dripping through the ashes in a separate
container (a by-product known as potash) and
then mixing together the potash and grease in a
cooking pot. Teeth can be cleaned with a twig by
separating the fibres at one end.

★ **Scavenge** – pick up anything that you see, you
never know when it could come in handy. Plastic
bags discarded by farmers can be used to store
items; birds' nests are great, as the eggs provide
a source of food and the nest can be used for
firewood. While resting up, collect earthworms and
insects in the immediate environment to consume
for energy.

★ **Treat injuries** – if an operator lets a wound fester
it could immobilise him, or even kill him. If the
operator was wounded during a contact prior to
the E&E procedure, he will need to treat the wound
urgently. If the wound is a capillary one, i.e. it does
not involve an artery or a vein, then it can be
controlled by applying pressure or creating a
tourniquet. More serious injuries will require expert
medical assistance.

In urban E&E situations, it's important to make sure
you look as inconspicuous as possible. Your body
language should be moderate and your appearance

When you're on the run it's all about mental strength. You're exhausted, and to know that you've got to hunt for each meal, sleep in a dirty, wet hide and constantly loop round on your movement requires huge mental strength and determination. Remember – the moment you get lazy is the moment you get caught.

indistinguishable from the man on the street. If the operator thinks he's being followed he will make for an underground station if possible, because the tunnel environment may block some radio comms. Jumping into taxis and asking to be driven to random destinations can throw a surveillance team. If the operator changes his appearance in a certain respect that can also confuse any trackers, for example shaving off a beard or dumping a brightly coloured piece of clothing. If the operator's accent is a dead giveaway then he will avoid speaking and therefore situations that would require him to talk. When travelling by car or on public transport, he will not take the most obvious journey, but instead build several red-herring tours into his trip to confuse any surveillance personnel.

SURVIVAL BELT

SF patrols need to carry E&E equipment in case the mission goes badly wrong. Once on an E&E manoevure they will have to forego protection and weaponry in favour of mobility. It's no good being pursued by the enemy if you're weighed down with a heavy machine gun. That said, there's still a load of equipment that operators can carry without adding too much of a load burden on to them. Every guy in the team will carry a survival belt that allows an operator on the run to stay operational for 48 hours. Gear that is included on a survival belt includes:

★ **Pistol**
★ **Knife**
★ **Ammo**
★ **Grenades** × 4 (two High-Explosive, one red, one green, two phosphorus — red smoke at an LZ tells the pilot above to back off, green instructs him that it's safe to land at the LZ)
★ **Halogen light bulb** (with fitted infrared lens that allows it to be seen from the air without being visible to nearby ground troops)
★ **Rifle cleaning kit** (including oil bottle)
★ **Water Bottles** × 2
★ **Water purification tablets**
★ **Hexi block** to make a fire
★ **Nails** × 3 to place the hexi block on
★ **Lightweight poncho** or **Gore-tex smock**
★ **Cord**
★ **Loop line** (to make a harness)
★ **Carabiner** (for use in the jungle when the soldier needs to use a winch system to extract)
★ **Candle**
★ **Matches**
★ **Small explosives**

- ★ **Det cord**
- ★ **Detonator**
- ★ **Mozzie cover**
- ★ **Cam cream**
- ★ **Wire saw** (to make shelters and traps)
- ★ **Leatherman tool**
- ★ **Emergency TACBE radio**
- ★ **Map**
- ★ **ID disc**
- ★ **Marker Panel** (to hold up and identify to aircraft)
- ★ **Basic medical kit** (field dressings etc)
- ★ **Blood coins** (for bribing locals)

In the event that the operator is captured and imprisoned, he will need to mentally prepare himself for interrogation, torture and imprisonment. His captors are unlikely to show him any mercy, but he can attempt to create a bond with his captor, for example by asking if the captor has kids, finding some common ground around which to build conversation and establish an emotional connection. The prisoner should never stare the interrogator directly in the eyes, and he should always be subservient. At the back of his mind, the operator should be thinking about how to escape. He'll keep a constant eye on what his interrogators and captors are doing without trying to look obvious.

You can have the most detailed E&E plan in the world, you can have all the equipment in the world, but when push comes to shove, what will really get you through an escape and evasion scenario is determination. It's not about morale, or remaining optimistic, or having courage: it's about being determined to do everything correctly, and see the job through to the end. Determination will make you cover your tracks and double-up to avoid trackers. Determination will keep you going when you're cold, hungry and tired. Forget guns or water purification tablets or a compass: determination is the one thing an operator can't survive without on an E&E manoeuvre.

FIGHT TO WIN

In an imprisonment scenario, tunnelling out of the camp is possible if the detainment area is a prisoner-of-war camp. If the operator is held in a traditional stone-cell prison he will have to use all his wits and planning to formulate an escape plan. Whether that is possible by killing a guard and stealing his uniform, encouraging a prison riot and escaping in the confusion, or even burrowing out over a period of time, really depends on the specific environment confronting the operator. In such a situation he needs to be very patient; some guys have had to survive for years in captivity before an escape opportunity has presented itself.

ELITE UNITS AROUND THE WORLD

18 (UKSF) SIGNALS REGIMENT / United Kingdom

18 Signals is composed of 264, SBS and 63 Signals, and is a specialist signals unit providing support to the Regiment. Its main remit is to provide signals intelligence, perform electronic intelligence and maintain comms security and integrity on SAS missions. Signals is a vital part of any SF operation and these guys will need to be able to accompany Blades on actual missions, so they need to be more than just a bit of a whizz with the computers and radios – they also need to be able to perform HALO freefalls, handle firearms expertly and have the same mental toughness and physical fitness levels as Regiment operators. To that end, 18 Signals run their own Selection programme called the Special Forces Communicator (SFC) course, which teaches them the

techniques of Special Forces operators alongside advanced signals training.

BOA (BUREAU OF COUNTER-TERRORIST OPERATIONS) / Poland

Poland's elite SWAT unit, BOA's role since 9/11 has been to suppress terrorist threats Poland has suffered at the hands of gangs and drug traffickers exploiting Poland's position as the gateway between Eastern and Western Europe. I got the chance to train with BOA recently – I was very impressed with what I saw. Experts in close-quarter combat and counter-terrorist assaults, BOA is trained by Poland's army special forces unit GROM.

BOPE (SPECIAL POLICE OPERATIONS BATTALION) / Brazil

BOPE is the elite paramilitary unit in Rio de Janeiro and specialise in urban combat. They are charged with bringing order and peace to the 900-odd favelas (shanty towns) that surround Rio's glamorous beaches and nightclubs. The favelas were created three hundred years ago when Brazil's freed slaves moved out of Rio and set up their own neighbourhoods. Now these have been taken over by gangs dealing in drugs, prostitution and gun crime, and it's down to BOPE to clean them up. They have to operate in close, restricted environments, against a hidden, violent enemy. Having worked alongside them, I know these guys mean business. Their badge – a knife through a skull – says it all.

DELTA FORCE / United States

Another unit that is heavily influenced by the Regiment, formed by Colonel Charles Beckwith after he was blown away by the intense training of the lads down in Hereford in the 1960s. Beckwith decided that the US needed a similar top-class unit and set them up in Fort Bragg, North Carolina. Unlike the Regiment, where you voluntarily apply for Selection, Delta Force monitors outstanding soldiers and sends them letters asking them to call a telephone number if they wish to apply. Delta operators take part in surveillance ops, hostage-rescue missions and snatching enemy targets for interrogation, and have played key roles in many missions down the years, such as the capturing of General Noriega in Panama during Operation Just Cause (1989). Just like Blades, Delta Forces tend to work in four-man patrols.

GROM (OPERATIONAL MOBILE REACTION GROUP) / Poland

A relatively new elite unit formed in the early 1990s and trained by my mates in the Regiment, GROM was designed to piece together soldiers from the many other Special Forces teams that had existed in Poland during the Cold War era, after the military chiefs realised one all-purpose unit was better than having several specialist forces teams with limited operational ability. They also lacked a counter-terrorist unit. GROM's founder and commander, Slawomir Petelicki, is a legendary figure among elite operators, with vast experience in sabotage and reconnaissance, and despite being the new kid on the scene, GROM has gained respect across the SF community for its operations.

GSG 9 (GRENZSCHUTZGRUPPE 9) / Germany

A lot of elite units are formed after a traumatic episode that reveals a nation's shortcomings in dealing with a particular type of threat. In the case of GSG 9, Germany's elite paramilitary police force, that tragedy was the massacre at the 1972 Munich Olympic Games. The government responded to the threat to its interior by creating GSG 9, and the unit is designed to deal with any type of terrorist threat. These guys have a very close relationship with the lads in Hereford, and just like the SAS, they have specialist maritime and airborne groups, along with operational and reserve counter-terrorism assault teams. Their finest hour was the successful assault on Lufthansa

Flight 181 aircraft at Mogadishu airport, and more recently they have been involved in operations apprehending terrorist suspects in Germany.

JUNGLA (ANTI-NARCOTICS JUNGLE COMPANY) / Colombia

Part of the Colombian National Police Force, the Junglas are one of a number of Special Groups created by the CNP to deal with specific threats to national security (others include the COPES quick reaction force and the ESMAD mobile riot squadron). The Junglas are trained in jungle survival techniques, able to live in the jungle for weeks on end, doing recces on enemy targets and carrying out assaults against suspected drug plantations. The main threat they face is from the numerous guerrilla groups active in the country – FARC, ELN and EPL, as well as the country's drug cartels. The Junglas worked alongside Colombia's other elite units, the Lanceros and the AFEU.

MAGAV (BORDER GUARD) / Israel

Charged with carrying out anti-terrorist operations in Israel, especially Jerusalem, and the occupied territories of the Gaza Strip and the West Bank, the Border Guards group draws its recruits from the Israel Defence Force (IDF) and has 8,000 operators in total. It has four Special Forces units rated amongst the best anti-terrorist units in the world. Yamam specialises in anti-terrorist and hostage-rescue operations, Yamas works undercover in the occupied territories, Matilan is an intelligence gathering unit and Yamag deals with counter-crime operations. The Magav often operate undercover in Palestinian-occupied territories – they have to be able to look and talk like the locals, and execute plans rapidly, because as soon as shots are fired, the surrounding environment will turn extremely hostile.

NAVY SEALs (SEA, AIR AND LAND FORCES) / United States

The SEALs were brought into active service in the 1960s, and specialise in maritime operations including reconnaissance work, riverine ops, sabotage, training and equipping foreign armies and guerrilla forces, and preventive and reactive counter-terrorism operations. There are 16 men to a SEAL platoon, although they tend to operate in groups half this size. SEALs have operated in a variety of combat theatres, from Vietnam through to present-day operations in Afghanistan and Iraq.

SAS (SPECIAL AIR SERVICE) / United Kingdom

The original and still the best. From its base in Hereford, the SAS, commonly known simply as 'the

Regiment' has proved time and again that its soldiers (also called Blades) are without equal in the world of elite operators and have lived up to their motto, 'Who Dares Wins'. The founder of the SAS was David Stirling, a colonel who organised covert operations against Axis forces in North Africa in the Second World War. The idea of a small, independent patrol carrying out attacks and surveillance deep behind enemy lines was hugely successful. Following the end of the war, the SAS cut its teeth in Malaya and Borneo, where the Regiment learned many of the techniques and SOPs that form the backbone of today's outfit, such as operating in four-man patrols and carrying out strategic assaults against large enemy forces.

The Regiment has seen action in more combat environments than any other elite team, giving it an edge when it comes to knowing what's required to succeed in virtually any situation operators are faced with. From jungle operations in Borneo through desert missions in Oman and Iraq, counter-terrorism ops in Northern Ireland and siege assaults in London, the SAS has the longest, proudest history of any SF group in the world. I'm proud to say I was a Blade.

SPECIAL AIR SERVICE REGIMENT / Australia
Created by the Aussies in the Second World War to launch operations against the Japanese behind

enemy lines, the SASR is closely modelled on the Regiment and is about 600-strong. Following the end of the war, the SASR cut its teeth working alongside British Blades in Borneo, and then alongside SEALs and US Army Special Forces in Vietnam. Based at Campbell Barracks in Swanbourne near Perth, the main role of the Oz SASR nowadays is counter-terrorism and surveillance. They work closely with other SF units around the world, including the Regiment and New Zealand SF, as well as elite operators in nearby Indonesia.

SBS (SPECIAL BOAT SERVICE) / United Kingdom

Based in Poole in Dorset, the SBS is the naval equivalent of the SAS and, like the Regiment, its history dates back to the Second World War, when special maritime units carried out raids against enemy coastline installations. The SBS used to deal strictly with maritime operations, but in recent years they have worked alongside the lads from Hereford in ground-based missions in Afghanistan and Iraq. Most famously they took part in the siege of the Qala-I-Jangi fort in Afghanistan after hundreds of captured al-Qaeda and Taleban fighters overpowered the guards. There were just six SBS operatives taking part in an assault against more than 300 insurgents armed to the teeth, but they succeeded in overpowering them – a testament to the SBS's fighting capabilities on land as well as sea.

SPECIAL FORCES BRIGADE /South Africa

Another unit to have worked very closely with the SAS. Commonly known as the 'Recces', the Special Forces Brigade have been involved in some seriously hardcore ops, including South Africa's long-running border wars with Namibia and Angola. Split into 4 Special Forces Regiment (maritime ops) and 5 Special Forces Regiment (land-based ops). Both groups specialise in reconnaissance work, carrying out covert operations and intelligence gathering. Counter-terrorism work is now part of the remit of the Special Task Force, a unit modelled on Germany's GSG 9.

SFSG (SPECIAL FORCES SUPPORT GROUP) / United Kingdom

The newest addition to UK SF, these guys are a quick reaction force that provides infantry support to the Regiment and the SBS. The lads are mostly drawn from 1 Para, with other guys joining from the Royal Marines and the RAF. SFSG consists of 4 Strike Companies (called A, B, C and F Company and comprised mainly of 1 Para with Royal Marines specialising in amphibious operations), 1 Support Company and the HQ Company. In addition, several units are attached to SFSG, such as the RAF Regiment's Forward Air Operators to provide close air support. The SFSG lads help to relieve the operational burden on the Regiment, allowing Blades to focus on direct action objectives and reducing the strain on the SF units during intensive combat operations.

(SRR) SPECIAL RECONNAISSANCE REGIMENT / United Kingdom

Stood up in April 2005 along with the SFSG and 18 Signals, the SRR is not a combat unit, but instead conducts surveillance operations mainly, but not limited to, counter-terrorist activities using hi-tech equipment to develop a level of intel that standard operational units would find it very difficult to achieve. Operating in Afghanistan and Iraq, it is the natural heir to 'The Det' (14 Intelligence Company), which worked as a surveillance and intel unit in Northern Ireland. Guys from the Regiment would serve tours of duty with The Det, providing them with the skill sets necessary to perfectly execute specialist surveillance operations.

SUNKAR / Kazakhstan

The Sunkar are Kazakhstan's elite paramilitary police unit, and they are trained to deal with counter-terrorism operations. Kazakhstan is a developing country and it faces risks both internally and externally, and Sunkar was created to anticipate and counter them. There are about 120 recruits in total. I had the chance to see them work up close recently, following them on a mission to track down a gang smuggling heroin. These guys are part of a relatively new force that is learning all the time, but I was very impressed with what I saw. Because of the country's Soviet past, Sunkar use a lot of Russian-manufactured weapons. They carry some serious firepower, including the thermobaric GM-94 grenade launcher and heavy machine guns, because they are dealing with a ruthless, violent enemy that is not interested in negotiations or surrender.

SPECIAL WARFARE GROUPS / China

Little is known about China's elite units, except that they were set up originally by parts of the Kuomintang Army that stayed on the mainland. They were trained by American paratroopers in airborne tactics after the Nationalists were defeated and fled to Taiwan. From this crude start point, Chinese SF groups have emerged, and today have several Special Forces groups that specialise in special reconnaissance missions and direct action operations. Each group has about 1,000 personnel attached and can operate in anything from two-man patrols (recces) through to large reinforced companies for counter-terrorism activities. Chinese elite operators are rumoured to have specialist equipment designed for elite operations, including a powered parachute that can take-off and land operators, with gear, across terrain quickly, and electronic systems that allow them to 'fingerprint' enemy radars. They tend to use Russian-designed weapons such as AK-47s and Dragunov sniper rifles.

SPETSNAZ (SPECIAL PURPOSE FORCES) / Russia

During the Cold War, Spetsnaz units were feared the world over. They were designed to provide 'diversionary reconnaissance' – acting as the lead force to recce key Western European targets ahead of a much larger ground invasion in the event of it all kicking off. When the Iron Curtain fell Spetsnaz briefly turned into a mess; however, when Putin came onto the scene he set about expanding the Spetsnaz units again to restore Russian military pride and might. Their role has changed from the Cold War to focus on special reconnaissance, operating in harsh environments such as Chechnya. Each Spetsnaz unit has eight to ten soldiers and operate in one of three types of unit: Razvedchiki (a battalion comprising an airborne company and a long range reconnaissance patrol company), Rejdoviki (carrying out recce ops, company or battalion-sized) and Vysotniki (closely resembling the SAS and working in 11-man teams). There are also Naval Spetsnaz outfits that operate alongside the Russian navy, designed to provide maritime reconnaissance.

STF (SPECIAL TASK FORCE) / Sri Lanka

Trained by the SAS, the STF is designed for counter-terrorism operations. Its main enemy is the Tamil Tigers, a highly mobile and well-equipped guerrilla army that has engulfed Sri Lanka in civil war for decades. Created in 1983, there are over 6,000 personnel in the STF, and their success in engaging and defeating the feared Tamil Tigers has meant that the STF is now one of the most respected elite units in the world, rightly considered experts in jungle warfare and counter-insurgency operations.

APPENDIX
ABBREVIATIONS

ABC	AUTOMATIC BRIGHTNESS CONTROL
AQT	AL-QAEDA/TALEBAN
BFT	BATTLE FITNESS TEST
BLS	BEACH LANDING SITE
BOA	BUREAU OF COUNTER-TERRORIST OPERATIONS (POLAND)
BOPE	SPECIAL POLICE OPERATIONS BATTALION (BRAZIL)
BUD/S	BASIC UNDERWATER DEMOLTION/SEAL SCREENING TEST
CCR	CLOSED CIRCUIT REBREATHER
CFT	COMBAT FITNESS TEST
CQB	CLOSE QUARTERS BATTLE
CSAR	COMBAT SEARCH AND RESCUE
CSEL	COMBAT SURVIVOR/EVADOR LOCATOR
DEBRA	DIVER'S ELECTRONIC BEACH RECONNAISSANCE AID
DPM	DISRUPTIVE PATTERN MATERIAL
DPV	DESERT PATROL VEHICLE
DVL	DOPPLER VELOCITY LOG
DZ	DROP ZONE
E&E	ESCAPE AND EVASION
EMLB	ENCLOSED MINE LIFT BAG

EOD	EXPLOSIVES ORDNANCE DISPOSAL
F&M	FIRE AND MOVEMENT
FAO	FORWARD AIR OPERATOR
FUP	FORMING-UP POINT
GPMG	GENERAL PURPOSE MACHINE GUN
GPS	GLOBAL POSITIONING SYSTEM
GROM	OPERATIONAL MOBILE REACTION GROUP (POLAND)
GSG-9	GRENSCHUTZGRUPPE-9 (GERMANY)
HAHO	HIGH ALTITUDE HIGH OPENING
HALO	HIGH ALTITUDE LOW OPENING
IED	IMPROVISED EXPLOSIVE DEVICE
LAW	LIGHT ANTI-ARMOUR WEAPON
LTD	LASER TARGET DESIGNATOR
LUP	LYING UP POINT
LZ	LANDING ZONE
MSHR	MINIATURE SECURE HANDHELD RADIO
Navy SEALs	NAVY SEA, AIR LAND
NBC	NUCLEAR, BIOLOGICAL, CHEMICAL
NVG	NIGHT VISION GOGGLES
OIC	OFFICER IN CHARGE
OP	OBSERVATION POST
PRR	PERSONAL ROLE RADIOS
REM	RAPID EYE MOVEMENT
RIBS	RIGID INFLATABLE BOATS
RPG	ROCKET PROPELLED GRENADE
RRC	RIGID RAIDING CRAFT
RTI	RESISTANCE TO INTERROGATION

RTU	RETURNED TO UNIT
RV	RENDEZVOUS
SAM	SURFACE TO AIR MISSILE
SAS	SPECIAL AIR SERVICE
SASR	SPECIAL AIR SERVICE REGIMENT (AUSTRALIA)
SBS	SPECIAL BOAT SERVICE (FORMERLY SPECIAL BOAT SQUADRON)
SDV	SWIMMER DELIVERY VEHICLE
SF	SUSTAINED FIRE
SFAS	SPECIAL FORCES ASSESSMENT AND SELECTION (UNITED STATES)
SFC	SPECIAL FORCES COMMUNICATOR COURSE
SIGINT	SIGNALS INTELLIGENCE
SOCR	SPECIAL OPERATIONS CRAFT RIVERINE
SOP	STANDARD OPERATING PROCEDURE
SPIE	SPECIAL PROCEDURES INSERTION AND EXTRACTION
SQT	SEAL QUALIFICATION TRAINING
SRR	SPECIAL RECONNAISSANCE REGIMENT
STABO	STABILIZED TACTICAL AIRBORNE BODY OPERATIONS
STF	SPECIAL TASK FORCE UNIT (SRI LANKA)
TACBE	TACTICAL BEACON
TEC	TAIL-END CHARLIE
TICM	THERMAL IMAGING COUNTERMEASURES
WMIK	WEAPONS MOUNTED INSTALLATION KIT

APPENDIX
ILLUSTRATIONS

Page 174   Harrier Jumpjet © Adrian Pingstone; image from
           http://commons.wikimedia.org

Page 175   Explosives operators © Crown Copyright/MOD. Reproduced
           with the permission of the Controller of Her Majesty's
           Stationery Office

Page 176   Bridge detonations © Mike Renwick

Page 179   US snipers © Pvt. Jennifer J. Eidson, US Department of
           Defense

Page 180   SEALs Woodlands ©US Department of Defense

Page 187   Sniper Afghanistan © US Department of Defense

Page 192   Room assault © Mike Renwick

Page 193   Multi-floor assault © Mike Renwick

Page 196   Bus assault © Mike Renwick

Page 207   River ©Adam J.W.C.; image from
           http://commons.wikimedia.org

Page 208   Wound © Sadeq Rahimi; image from
           http://commons.wikimedia.org

Page 214   Horn of Africa walking Zodiac © Tech. Sgt. Jeremy T. Lock,
           U.S. Air Force; image from http://commons.wikimedia.org

Page 215   Green Berets © Sgt. Matthew S. Friberg, U.S. Army; image
           from http://commons.wikimedia.org

Page 219   Chinook © Adrian Pingstone; image from
           http://commons.wikimedia.org

INDEX